Dear Home

Fred Roberts, Mabel Wait Roberts, and Gladys Wait Roberts, c. 1912

Dear Home

The 1901 and 1902 Diary of Mabel Lila Wait

Edited by

Susan Ward

Friends of the Owen D. Young Library
St. Lawrence University
Canton, N.Y.

This publication would not have been possible without the help of a great many people. Principal among them are Catherine Cady Davis, Mabel's granddaughter who first shared Mabel's diary with me; Herbert and Mary Ruth Judd, whose memories of Canton history and of Mabel were an invaluable resource; George Gibson, whose advice on working with diaries was wise and helpful; and Shirley Tramontana, whose knowledge of the period was extremely useful and who also opened the resources of the St. Lawrence County Historical Society to me. The St. Lawrence University Faculty Research Fund awarded me a grant that made much of the research and preparation of this manuscript possible. Acknowledgments are also due to Frances Weller Bailey, Neal Burdick, Marnie Crowell, Lynn Case Ekfelt, William Elberty, Diane Exoo, Joyce Freitag, Peter Freitag, Albert Glover, Bart Harloe, John Jaunzems, Darlene Leonard, Richard Kuhta, Nimanthi Rajasingham, Tim Wright, and the entire staff at the St. Lawrence County Historical Society. For all your help, many thanks.

**Designed and typeset by
John N. Serio**

Cover design and photograph reproductions by
Faye A. Serio

Distributed by
Syracuse University Press
Syracuse, N.Y. 13244 USA

ISBN 0-9634028-3-8 (pbk. : alk. paper)

"If I can only keep my dear home."

Memoranda, 1901
—Mabel Lila Wait

Contents

ã Introduction ã

Mabel Lila Wait was an ordinary young woman from upstate New York who did an extraordinary thing. In 1901, over the opposition of her brother and most of her other male relatives, she drove to town, took out a mortgage, and bought the family farm. While farm ownership by a single woman was not in itself so unusual, Mabel's intent to run the farm by herself was. She came from a class of people who did not believe that running a farm was the business of women. Her father, Marvin Wait, was a prominent citizen in Canton, the county seat. He had been a founding member of the St. Lawrence County Board of Trade, which regulated the prices of dairy products, an important position in a dairying area, and a clerk in the State Assembly in Albany for several years. He is described by neighbors who remember the family as a "prosperous" farmer, and he was a prominent enough citizen to be listed in an 1878 edition of the county history.[1] The women in Marvin Wait's family did household chores, but they did not consider farm chores suitable work. Mabel's decision to take over the family farm thus makes her seem unusually "liberated" for the period, the region, and the class in which she lived.

Mabel's transformation into a farm owner and manager forms an important "plot" in the diary. By the time both her parents died, she was twenty-four, single, and needed a place to live. Her father's will, when it was probated in 1900, had left the farm equally to Mabel, her brother Mert, and her married sister Edith, who lived with her family in Maine. It included the proviso that their mother could enjoy the farm and all the benefits of the property so long as she remained alive. But Mrs. Wait died in February 1901, and Mert, who had been living with his new wife in half of the Wait farmhouse and doing the heavy work of the farm, wanted to try some other livelihood. He pressed Mabel to sell the farm and split the profits. Mabel, who was attached to the farm and to her parents' memory, refused to do so. She went to see the family lawyer and convinced him to secure the property so that it could not be sold without her consent. Then she set about procuring a mortgage and, with her older sister's compliance, quite literally bought Mert out.

Records in the St. Lawrence County Clerk's office reveal that Mabel convinced her sister Edith, who seems to have had no wish to oppose Mabel's notion to take over the farm, to co-sign a mortgage allowing her to buy Mert out of his one-third share of the farm. Mabel took out a mortgage for $1500, negotiated with St. Lawrence University, which, at that time, kept some of its assets in real estate. She seems to have had little trouble doing business with lawyers and mortgage agents. Within a few weeks of taking over the farm, she also took over, quite capably, the family business interests, assuming responsibility for the farm insurance, the blacksmith's and grain miller's bills, and all debts connected with her parents' illnesses. She became suddenly conscious of the price of groceries, engaged a man to fix the roof, paid the hired man, and calculated what the fall threshers cost in terms of food and labor. She seems to have moved easily into the masculine sphere of managing money as well as that of owning a farm.

But Mabel's diary reveals her internal turmoil as she tried to determine the best course of action. Women in the Wait household had churned butter, fed the hens, and traded eggs for groceries, but that was as far as they had ventured into the work of the farm on a daily basis. Mabel did not, as one of her descendants wrote, "like to get her hands dirty," and she preferred to leave the daily farm chores to "the boys," as she called the male family members or the hired men who performed them. There is some indication in an earlier diary that she regarded even the hitching up or stabling of a horse she had driven to town and back as something she ought not to be doing. She wanted to keep on in the same pattern.

This attitude led to a social predicament. The Waits had often employed hired men, and Mabel had no trouble finding someone to do the farm work. But a young unmarried woman living alone on a farm with a hired man might cause neighbors and family to talk. Mabel was not insensible to this probability. She took care to invite friends from town or female relatives or neighboring farm girls to stay overnight with her as often as possible, and she quickly engaged her cousin, Bert Earl, and his wife, Lula, to live in the other half of the house so that Bert could take over the farm chores. The night before Bert and Lula arrived, she wrote in her diary: "Guy [the hired man] staid in the horse barn. I am glad I haven't got to stay alone here much longer" (Oct. 17, 1901). Her relief was evident.

Her position as a single young woman who owned a farm also made the marriage question more pressing. Marriage would have solved the problem of finding a man to do the chores, and Mabel would have provided a good catch for a single young man without property. But Mabel seems to have had little inclination to marry hastily. Her diary before her parents' deaths indicates she was attractive and attracted to a number of young men. It also reveals that she had had at least one serious suitor, Fred

Roberts, a schoolteacher from Potsdam, whom she had met while taking part in a Grange play in 1900. Roberts became a constant caller and supported Mabel and her mother through her father's death and funeral in May 1900. In June, he seems to have proposed to her, causing her to write: "I wish things were different. I don't know what to do. It was a shame to make him feel bad after he has been so kind to me" (June 18, 1900). Though he left the area that summer to settle in the midwest, he wrote to her almost daily, and his letters added motivation for her frequent trips to the corner mailbox. Roberts, though far away, was an important presence in Mabel's life in 1901 and 1902. His letters, always noted in the diary, often "did [her] lots of good," and, when they failed to arrive, caused her to comment that she "wonder[ed] what was the matter."

But in December of 1901, soon after Bert and Lula Earl moved to the farm, Lula's brother, Charlie Nichols, arrived to help with the farm work. He remained on the farm until the beginning of April, and he and Mabel grew close. A month-long visit to her cousins in Ogdensburg in May put Mabel into close contact with Nichols again, and he visited her several times during the summer. Charlie Nichols undoubtedly helped to keep her feelings of loneliness at bay during the period of adjustment her mother's death and brother's desertion ushered in. He also confounded her feelings about Fred Roberts. Mabel's feelings about both suitors and her eventual decision to accept one of them form a second "plot" in the diary.

At the same time that the diary tells the story of a determined young woman, it also discloses a good deal about late-nineteenth-century rural work patterns, particularly those of rural women. As a prosperous dairy farmer, Marvin Wait had owned a farm of 120 acres with approximately 40 to 50 cows.[2] At the time of his death, there were at least two barns on the farm: a horse barn and a cow barn. Besides the cows and horses, there were chickens, ducks, and pigs to feed, feed grain to plant, cultivate and harvest, and wood to chop and haul from the family wood lot to fuel the several individual stoves that heated the house and were the basis for the family's cooking. Cows were milked twice a day, and the milk was taken in cans to a "factory" in the neighborhood, where it was processed into cheese.[3] The men did most of these chores. The women in the household fed the chickens and ducks, collected eggs, and churned a small amount of milk into butter which they sent to the factory to be sold. Aside from these activities, their typical day might include cooking, sweeping, mopping, dusting, preserving fruits and vegetables, washing clothes, mending, doing patchwork or making rag rugs.[4] Mabel's diary records her doing all of these things, both before and after her parents' deaths.

The diary also suggests much about the social life and attitudes of unmarried middle-class women of the period. Whatever else she was before the death of her parents, Mabel was a young woman in her early twenties who enjoyed going out and flirting with various young men and who looked forward, at some distant time, to marrying and settling down to a life that reflected the life of her middle-class parents. Before her parents' deaths, after doing her share of the household chores, she drove into town to shop and visit with girlfriends. She went to plays and lectures, became involved with amateur theatricals, went to church and Grange socials, visited for periods of a few days to a few weeks with cousins in nearby towns, and spent long hours writing letters and making entries in her diary. She noted with interest encounters with good looking young men, but she did not seem to favor any one of them. All this would seem to suggest a lack of interest in the domestic. On the other hand, she loved children and she enjoyed taking care of both Maud, her niece, and Lou, Bert's daughter, when each lived in the "other part" of the house. She toiled over scrapbooks, Christmas stockings, and doll clothes for her small nieces and nephew. She did patchwork and fancy needlework and maintained an extensive flower garden. She kept a recipe book. She noted particular feats of cookery or housewifery with satisfaction in her diary. She reflected the domestic attitudes of the "Ladies' Home Journal," whose pages she avidly read. In short, Mabel was a blend of the attitudes of the independent New Woman and the Victorian girl whose proper business was to prepare herself to take over the role of wife and mother.[5]

Mabel's disinclination to marry at a young age was not atypical of a subgroup of young women of the period. In her study of American girlhood in the nineteenth century, Barbara Welter discusses young women who were particularly attached to their fathers as being disinclined to leave home,[6] and Mabel fits this pattern. Before her parents' deaths, she seemed to cling to the position of younger daughter, feeling pleased when her mother returned from the village with a new shirtwaist for her, crying when she heard the news of her brother's impending wedding, feeling sad when she was told she must dismantle her childhood playroom to make room for a new "sleeping chamber." Her attachment to her father, who suffered from a chronic illness, is evident in this entry from her diary of 1899:

> This afternoon I was sitting in the sitting room looking out
> of the window and feeling sad. Papa came up and kissed me
> and asked me why I was so sober. He said he didn't like to see
> me sad. In all of his suffering, he sympathizes with me.

Parents and family were clearly the center of her world. Known family members are listed in the genealogy in Appendix A.

After her parents' deaths and her purchase of the farm, Mabel struggled to retain the status quo. Her daily round of activities did not change; she still churned butter for her "butter jar," did the daily round of sweeping, dusting, mopping, etc., with extra cleaning added on Saturdays, cooked, baked, and preserved, did fancy patchwork, and wrote diary entries and letters. She still walked eagerly to the corner mailbox to see who had answered her letters and still recorded encounters with nice looking young men when she went to town. But her life, inevitably, changed. Her concern with family translated into loneliness. She missed her role as daughter. Her arguments with Mert, who was her adored older brother, left her badly shaken. Her daily writing took the place of family conversations. And she was sensitive to the comments of relatives and neighbors on what she called her "position," noting in her diary after a report of an aunt's criticism: "it makes me so angry" (July 30, 1902).

Mabel Wait's diary of 1901 and 1902 thus has much to tell us. It relates the story of a determined young woman who did an unusual thing, but it also discloses what life was like for women in general in a small town in rural New York State at the beginning of the twentieth century. Mabel's world, a world of patchwork quilts, kerosene lamps, chimney fires, moonlit buggy rides, neighbors and relatives, weddings and funerals, trips to town to consult the lawyer and trips to town to see the latest show at the Opera House, is all contained within these pages. Mabel's diary brings this world, as well as Mabel herself, alive for us. Its ability to do so, perhaps, is the best reason for reading it.

A Note on the Text

There is much evidence that Mabel Wait kept a diary throughout a large portion of her adult life. She mentions diary writing as a regular part of her day at various times, and gifts of diaries for the coming years from her father in 1900 and from Fred Roberts in 1901 suggest that her diary keeping was a long established practice. Her daughter also confirmed the picture of Mabel as a regular diary writer. Mabel saved all her diaries, but many of them were lost in a house fire in 1938. Diaries from 1899, 1900, 1901, 1902, 1903, 1906, 1908, and 1917 were saved and afford glimpses into Mabel's life and into the life of the time and place in which she lived.

Diary writing among young women was a popular practice in the latter part of the nineteenth century, and Mabel may have begun her diary simply to follow a fad. Her diary suggests, however, that her daily entries became important as records of what happened to her and to members of her family; in at least one instance, she talks about looking over her diary to find out something she wanted to remember (July 2, 1902). Particularly in the years 1901 and 1902, when she was recovering from the deaths of her parents and her brother's departure, letter and diary writing helped to assuage her loneliness. "I wrote nearly all day," she noted on June 2, 1901. "I was very lonely. If it hadn't been for my writing, I don't know what I would have done." All of these motivations for writing place Mabel squarely in the middle of a tradition of diary keeping peculiar to American women of the late nineteenth and early twentieth centuries.[7]

Mabel's subjects vary, of course, according to the year. Her overriding subjects in 1901 and 1902 were her parents' deaths, her loneliness, the purchase of the farm, and her decisions about marriage. Sets of recurring images reinforce these subjects: visits to her parents' graves, daily walks to the corner mailbox, frequent trips to town to consult the family lawyer, Mabel happy at a visit or a letter, and Mabel lonely because she has no one to talk to. In 1902, as she shouldered the financial responsibilities of the household and the farm, money became a frequent subject. In that year, she began to use the space under her daily entries to record expenses, and it is interesting to note the changeover from expenditures for postage and hair ribbons recorded at the back of the 1901 diary to expenditures for lemons, shoes, bananas, and beef recorded after the daily entries in 1902. Her concern over money during 1902 is plain in this entry, in which she totaled up her May expenses. "53 cts. for May," she wrote on May 31, 1902, after spending the month with cousins in Ogdensburg. "Only 53 cts. And yet I had the finest time all the month. But somebody else paid the bills." Although Mabel's expenses are not reprinted here, a sample of monthly expenses from both years is reproduced in Appendix B.

A notable feature of Mabel's diary is what she leaves out. Mabel's main interest was her family and those with whom she was in close contact. Like many women diarists, she wrote about them to the exclusion of events of public import. A good example of an ignored public event is the assassination of President William McKinley in September 1901. McKinley was shot at the Pan American Exhibition in Buffalo on September 6 and died eight days later. The *Plaindealer*, the local Canton newspaper that Mabel read regularly, carried running reports of the President's condition. But during this period, Mabel was preoccupied with obtaining a mortgage to buy Mert out of his share of the farm. "Mert came up here and he and Lena and I went to the village," she wrote on September 14, 1902, the day the

President died. "Mert and I stayed all day to fix up our business, and we have agreed to settle at Mert's price. That is a relief to me." The assassination of the President is never mentioned in any entry. Another subject Mabel ignored was Fred Roberts' life as a schoolteacher. Roberts had worked hard to put himself through Potsdam Normal School in order to become a teacher, and he taught school for most of his adult life. But in the extant volumes of her diary, there is only one mention of his profession, when Mabel notes that someone had asked him to consider taking a school in the Brick Chapel area. Her focus on Roberts' farm work to the exclusion of his professional life as a teacher underscores once again her intense concentration on the farm and the personal affairs of her family and friends.

Mabel also included hints of incidents, enclosed in parentheses, she wanted to remember but did not want to record in full. The subjects of many of these incidents were encounters with young men. Whether she felt uncomfortable writing about certain subjects or whether she was, in fact, cautious about the possibility of the diary's becoming a record for eyes besides her own, her reticence and her practice of including oblique references is in keeping with the practice of many other women diarists of this and later periods.

Mabel's writing style was terse, but not so terse as that of many rural diarists. She always began with the weather, but this was a common practice among rural people and also a procedure recommended by at least one nineteenth-century writer offering advice to young women diarists.[8] Her diary is filled with colloquial expressions: the hired man is "over to" the barn, she gets the house "slicked up," and, when it snows hard, it snows "like everything." Still, Mabel had an eye for detail and she wrote well. She used at least one Latin phrase in the diary, suggesting she had had at least some high school education, probably at the Canton Union School which offered studies in Classics. Her spelling is in keeping with the spelling of the period.

Mabel Wait's 1901 and 1902 diary was written in ink in small diary books, approximately 4 inches by 6 inches. This edition is as verbatim a transcription as conditions would allow. Whenever possible, Mabel's original grammar, spelling, and punctuation have been preserved. To avoid confusion, proper names have been spelled consistently throughout. The original of the 1901 diary and a photocopy of the 1902 diary are in the St. Lawrence University Archives.

Tuesday, January 1, 1901

Pleasant and cold
and a beautiful
moonlight night.
I staied at home
all day. Mama
and I had a
good but simple
dinner. I helped
do the housework
in the forenoon
and finished
up my diary for
1900 in the afternoon
and put it away.
My dear little
diary almost the
last present from
the dearest of
fathers. And this
diary is dear
to me too. I hope
pleasant things
can be written

🐦 1901 🐦

JANUARY

Tuesday, Jan. 1   Pleasant and cold and a beautiful moonlight night. I staid at home all day. Mama and I had a good but simple dinner. I helped do the housework in the forenoon and finished up my diary for 1900 in the afternoon and put it away. My dear little diary, almost the last present from the dearest of fathers.[1] And this diary is dear to me, too. I hope pleasant things can be written in it.

Wednesday, Jan. 2   Pleasant and real cold. Snowed some. Another lovely night. I ironed some last evening and some today. I also did some house work today and mended some. I got a beautiful letter from Mr. Roberts.[2] We got nice letters from Edith[3] and Ed Ryder too. I also got a paper from Mr. R.[4] Don't know what I'd do without the fine letters I get. They do me so much good.

Thursday, Jan. 3   Pleasant but very cold. I did quite a lot of odd jobs getting ready to go back to Norwood[5] Saturday night. Another beautiful moonlight night. Mama popped another pan of corn last night. Mert went to the village in the afternoon. I sent for a new puff comb by him.

Friday, Jan. 4   Quite pleasant but it snowed some. We all got up between 3 & 4 o'clock this morning for Irma was taken sick.[6] Mert went after her mother and the doctor, and about two in the afternoon little Maud Lorraine was born. Mert is very proud of her. Irma got along very nicely. In the evening I went up to the Mills[7] to the Foresters[8] supper and installation of officers with Zuar.[9] I had a fine time and a great visit with Mr. Hubbard.

Saturday, Jan. 5   Pleasant and cold. I did up the work for Mama, for she staid up stairs with Irma and the baby so Mrs. Wood could wash. Aunt Laurinda came over to stay all night and Uncle Nelson and Aunt Louise[10] were down to see the baby. I got a lovely letter from Mr. Roberts and Mama and Mert both got nice letters from Edith. Mama got a postal from Aunt Mercy. Mert carried me down town to take the 6:37 train for

Norwood. There were lots of people on the cars. They all seemed glad to see me here in Norwood.

Sunday, Jan. 6   Pleasant. Em, Edie[11] and I went to church in the morning. I wanted to go in the evening but didn't. I wrote to Edith and Mr. Roberts in the afternoon. I read some. They had callers here in the afternoon, Mrs. Nickerson and Mrs. Harwell. Fred[12] carried on in the evening like everything and kept us all laughing.

Monday, Jan. 7   Pleasant, snowed some. I ironed all the afternoon. Edith brought home a girlfriend to supper. Em popped corn in the evening. I got another present from Mr. Roberts today, a memoranda tablet-calendar. It is pretty nice.

Tuesday, Jan. 8   Very pleasant in the forenoon, grew cloudy in the afternoon and rained in the evening. Net, Hazel, and Pauline were here in the afternoon. Eva and Will were both in for a few minutes. This is Fred's birthday. He is 14 years old. They invited Harry and Charlie Cassada here to supper, and Alta Marsh came home with Edie and was here too. Had a nice supper. I went over street twice after the mail. My letters didn't come tonight.

Wednesday, Jan. 9   Pleasant. I didn't have so very much work to do. Got it all done in the forenoon and sat down in the afternoon and read some and played games with Hazel. She was here all day. She was here all day for her folks went to Buck's Bridge.[13] Em was up to Mr. Mott's all day. I got a letter from Edith but Mr. R.'s letter didn't come today. I went over to the post office in the evening. (Our early caller and the trip. When did you come?)

Thursday, Jan. 10   Snowed most all day. I got the work all done up in the forenoon and read in the afternoon. (Our groceries that had to be brought up in the afternoon. "I didn't know I was in such demand.") I went for a ride around town with Fred and called at Mr. Mott's and went up stairs to see Ida. She is sick. I got my letter from Mr. Roberts that I have been looking for and got a letter from Mama.

Friday, Jan. 11   Snowed in the forenoon, stopped in the afternoon and snowed again in the evening. I got the work done up in the forenoon and wrote to Mama in the afternoon and did some work. Mr. and Mrs. Mott, Mrs. Nickerson, Will, Hazel and Pauline called in the afternoon. Edith, Fred and I all went in a load down to Louisville[14] to a play in the evening, 15 in the load. Such a time. We were nearly frozen when we got back about 4 o'clock in the morning. I had an awful headache, was very tired and cold. Mr. Avery.

Saturday, Jan. 12   Snowed and drifted all day and the wind blew hard. Got up at 8 and helped do the work and went to bed again in the afternoon and had a good sleep. I was so tired. The roads were drifted awfully when we came home last night or this morning, nine teams came back in a row. I got a fine letter from Mr. Roberts and one from Edith. I read a little in the evening and took a bath and went to bed then. (Haven't those people got up yet?)

Sunday, Jan. 13   Pleasant. Edith and I went to church and stayed a while to Sunday school and then went over to Mr. Mott's to call, then came home and ate dinner and went for a ride all around town in the afternoon alone. Mrs. Nickerson and Mrs. Adams both called in the afternoon. Edith read part of "The Yankee Detective"[15] in the afternoon. We went to church in the evening, Epsworth League and church. (The young gentlemen behind us and what Fred heard them say about me.)

Monday, Jan. 14   A beautiful day. We did a great big washing and I mopped, besides the common work.[16] I was tired and went to bed early. Will, Hat, and the baby were down in the afternoon. I got a letter from Mama and one from Mabel Lewis. Mr. and Mrs. Mott called too in the afternoon. The clothes got dry today and Aunt Mercy brought them in, the first time they have dried good since I have been here.

Tuesday, Jan. 15   Snowed a little most all day but wasn't cold. I ironed some in the afternoon. Laid down a while. I got a letter from Edith that made me feel sad because she was feeling so sad, one from Mr. Roberts that was jolly. I wrote a long letter to Mama and had a great time with my fountain pen. It seemed to be stopped up some way so it didn't work good but it worked all right tonight when I began to write.

Wednesday, Jan. 16   It was cloudy in the morning and rained quite hard, but in the afternoon the sun shone. I ironed quite a bit. My pen works all right tonight and I am so glad. I wrote two letters tonight. Got a paper from Mr. Roberts.

Thursday, Jan. 17   Pleasant. The wind blew hard. Mr. Pitt called here, old Mr. Pitt. I swept and dusted the chambers, mopped and finished the ironing besides the common work. Mrs. Adams called. I was tired and was going to bed early but Edie kept me up and we staid awake after we went to bed until all hours, carrying on.

Friday, Jan. 18   Very cold but pleasant. Mr. Reed was here to dinner. I got a letter from Mama and one from Edith. Aunt Mercy, Edie and I went to a play, "Tony the Convict,"[17] in the evening. Fred went too. The play was fine. It is after eleven now, and I have got to write a letter to Mama yet before I go to bed.

Saturday, Jan. 19   Pleasant and very cold. (Our early visitor.) Dolph and Net drove down, got here just before dinner and started back about 5 o'clock. I felt bad and homesick and everything else. I went to bed early and had a good sleep. They were all out in the evening except Uncle Allen, Aunt Mercy and I.

Sunday, Jan. 20   Pleasant. I didn't go to church in the morning, for we were late getting up and the work was late. I went over to the post office at noon to see if I had a letter for no one went last night after the evening train came in, but I didn't get any letters. Fred, Edie and I went for a ride in the afternoon. Em, Edie and I went over to Mr. and Mrs. Mott's about 4 o'clock. Edie and I staid until church time and then went to church. Miss Lytle and Mr. Bonham were at Mr. Mott's.

Monday, Jan. 21   Pleasant and quite mild. We did a big washing and I mopped. I was tired and my back ached. I laid down a while in the afternoon. Edith was at home all day and amused me part of the time. I made molasses candy in the evening and Edith and I pulled it. Had splendid luck. It was just fine. I got a letter from Mama.

Tuesday, Jan. 22   Cold again. I began to feel sick just before dinner. I laid down all the afternoon. Got a letter from Mr. Roberts. I went to bed or laid down this afternoon at about 1:30 and didn't get up until dusk and about the first thing I saw was the new moon out of the window.

Wednesday, Jan. 23   Pleasant and cold. I did up the common work and ironed in the afternoon and wrote a letter to Mama. (The team that drove in this afternoon.) I got a letter from Edith and both of the dear little babies were sick and she was most sick. I will be so worried about them. I wrote to Edith too this afternoon.

Thursday, Jan. 24   Pleasant. I mended most all the afternoon. I came up stairs after the work was done up and read quite a while. Ethel

Barnes and Frances Clark were in here with Edie. Edie staid all night with the Clark girl.

Friday, Jan. 25   Pleasant. I did the common work and ironed a mess of starched clothes in the afternoon. Mrs. Adams called in the afternoon. I got a letter from Mama and one from Mr. Roberts. I went to "Uncle Tom's Cabin"[18] in the evening with Aunt Mercy. It was very good. We had to stop and buy some butter.

Saturday, Jan. 26   A beautiful day. I worked all the forenoon and did up the work after dinner. Then Edie and I called into Mrs. Mowett's and then went up to Will's. We staid until supper time. Supper was ready when we got back. Eva came back with us and staid to supper. Edie and Eva were vaccinated after supper. I got a letter from Edith, a lot of their Lenten programs[19] and a paper from Mr. Roberts. The babies were a little better.

Sunday, Jan. 27   Very pleasant. I staid in all day except to go for a ride with Fred in the afternoon. Had a nice ride. Uncle Allen and Aunt Mercy went up to Will's. Mrs. Adams was down in the afternoon. I feel tired and sad and lonely and homesick.

Monday, Jan. 28   It snowed and was cold and the wind blew all day. We did a big washing. I laid down a while in the afternoon. Got a letter from Mama and one from Edith. The babies are better. I am so glad. Ethel Barnes and Frances Clark came home with Edie and staid to supper.

Tuesday, Jan. 29   Pleasant and real cold. I worked most all day. Came up stairs in the afternoon and read the letters that I have here that Mr. R. wrote. I got a letter from Edith. They are better and I am so glad.

Wednesday, Jan. 30   Very pleasant. I worked all day and was very tired and my back ached so hard. I got a fine letter from Mr. Roberts and a paper. I am going to write to Edith tonight and to Mr. R. but what can I say to him after the letter I got from him?

Thursday, Jan. 31   Pleasant. I worked all the forenoon. I washed the dishes after dinner, there was a great big batch of them. I was so tired I could hardly stand it. I came up stairs and laid down and went to sleep. Got up about supper time, got supper and finished the ironing. Mr. Drury came here, staid to dinner and in the afternoon. Then he went up to Mr. Barnes. I got a letter from Mama. I went to bed early and had a fine sleep all night.

FEBRUARY

Friday, Feb. 1　　　　　Pleasant but it snowed a little. I got the work mostly done in the forenoon. I mended my waist in the afternoon. Em and I called at Mrs. Adams in the afternoon. She showed me all of her paintings. Edie and I called at Mrs. Nickerson's after supper. I got a letter from Edith. Mr. Drury came back here and went home on the 3:20 train.

Saturday, Feb. 2　　　　　Very pleasant both day and night. I worked all the forenoon, slicked up in the afternoon and went over street with Edie and Eva. Then Edie and I called on Ellis Nickerson. My letter didn't come and I could have cried. Will's folks went to Mert Beswick's wedding in the evening, and Aunt Mercy went up and staid with the children. I took a bath in the evening and then read quite a while.

Sunday, Feb. 3　　　　　Very pleasant. Aunt Mercy, Edie, and I went to church and Sunday School. Edie, Fred and I went for a ride in the afternoon. I wrote to Edith and Mr. R. when I got back. Edie and I went to the Congregational church in the evening. We sat back with the "rest of the boys." Mr. Avery sat right behind me. Mr. Bonham was to Sunday School. Mr. and Mrs. Adams stopped here on their way home from church.

Monday, Feb. 4　　　　　It snowed all day. I helped about the work. Finished reading my book in the afternoon that I have been reading. I got a letter from Mama.

Tuesday, Feb. 5　　　　　Real cold but pleasant. I helped about the work. Edie was sick. Mr. and Mrs. Mott were over in the afternoon a while and Mrs. Adams. I got a letter from Edith and one from Mr. Roberts.

Wednesday, Feb. 6　　　　　Cold and pleasant. I helped do up the work in the forenoon. Aunt Mercy and I went up to school to Rhetoricals in the afternoon. Will carried us up. We went shopping a little while. I wrote two letters in the forenoon and picked up my things. Ida came over. Fred, Ida and I went for a ride all around town before supper. We had popcorn in the evening and Harry Cassada was here to see Edie.

Thursday, Feb. 7　　　　　Pleasant and cold. I helped do up the work. In the afternoon Em and I went over to the church to the W.C.T.U. Convention.[20] Will carried us over. I staid until between 4 & 5 then Edie and I went up to Hat's. We staid to supper and Hat and Eva went back to the church with us to the evening session. I got a paper from Mr. R.

Friday, Feb. 8   I got everything ready to come home. It was pleasant and cold. Marnie Mott came down on the noon train. We slept three in a bed, Marnie, Edie and I. In the afternoon Em and I went over to the church again and stopped at the depot to see the 3:20 train off. (Chocolates.) Then we went down street in the evening. (What the children had to tell me.)

Saturday, Feb. 9   Pleasant in the forenoon, snowed like everything in the afternoon. I came home on the noon train. Mert was down town to meet me. It was real cold. Mrs. Adams came down to bid me good bye. The baby seemed glad to see me. I got a letter and paper from Mr. R. I slept so good in my own bed, hardly stirred until morning.

Sunday, Feb. 10   Very pleasant. Willie Winslow came up in the morning. He ate dinner with Mama and me. Mert, Irma and the baby went down to Mr. Carter's[21] to dinner. Little Maud has been in our part quite a good deal today. We popped a big pan full of corn this afternoon, Mama and I. I wrote my letters and read some. (The two Mr. Pooles.)

Monday, Feb. 11   Very pleasant. I picked up a lot of pretty pieces to make a sofa pillow and ironed them out. Mert and Irma went to the village. The baby stayed with us. She was real good. Fred Mead and his wife called to see the baby.[22]

Tuesday, Feb. 12   Quite pleasant. Snowed some, and in the evening the wind blew. The baby was in our part all day. Mert went to the village toward night and Irma ate supper with us. I looked up some more pieces and nearly made one side of my sofa pillow.

Wednesday, Feb. 13   Cold and windy but pleasant. I got a letter from Edith and one from Mr. R. The letter I got from him surprised me very much and didn't make me feel good at all. I have written three letters today. Little Maud has been in here all day as she is every day nearly. She is a cute little thing. Mert got three valentines last night for me to give to the babies.

Thursday, Feb. 14   Cold and pleasant. I worked on my crazy sofa pillow. Mrs. Carter brought Anna Barnes Smithers up here to see Irma. She came into our part in the afternoon and visited quite a while. I went to bed early and had a good sleep. Little Maud was in here all day.

Friday, Feb. 15   Cold, quite pleasant. Mert carried Anna down town in the forenoon. Guy was here to help Mert draw hay. Poor Mama was taken sick about noon, in awful pain. She grew worse all the afternoon and vomited six times.[23] I was awfully frightened. Mert went for the doctor about 4 o'clock. He left some medicine so she rested some. I staid up all night with her and gave her medicine. We got a letter from Edith and I got one from Mr. R. that was better than the last one.

Saturday, Feb. 16   Very pleasant and much warmer. Mama began to grow worse again and was in terrible pain. Mert went for the doctor again in the forenoon but neither he or the doctor got here until between 4 & 5 o'clock at night. I was so tired and nervous in the afternoon with Mama so bad and no one to do anything but myself. I got another letter from Mr. R. and we got another from Edith.

Sunday, Feb. 17   Very pleasant and quite warm. Guy stopped here and Mert asked him to bring Aunt Laurinda over so he did about noon. Mama was awful bad all day. I tried to lie down and get some rest in the afternoon but couldn't for she was suffering so. The doctor came up twice, gave her an injection of morphine and left it for me to do through the night. How I dreaded it but I kept her easy. Aunt Laurinda staid up until about 11:30, then I got up.

Monday, Feb. 18   Pleasant and mild. I laid down in the forenoon and staid until between 2 & 3 o'clock. Then Mert and I drove up to the Mills to change some eggs for some groceries.[24] I enjoyed the ride. This has been the best day Mama has had. I sat up until 12 then Irma got up. They took baby down to her mother's to stay a few days so Irma could help me. The fore part of the night Mama slept good. I read her some stories. Some of the neighbors call every day.

Tuesday, Feb. 19   Pleasant. The latter part of last night Mama vomited the most of the time. She was fairly comfortable through the day. I sat up until 1:30 then Irma got up. Mama slept pretty good the fore part of the night. I wrote to Edith and Mr. R. and read eight chapters in "Malcolm Kirk."[25] Some more of the neighbors called. I was sick part of the time but I kept up. Mert has a hard cold. Guy came over to do the chores for him so he could doctor up.

Wednesday, Feb. 20   Pleasant but colder. More of the neighbors called. Mama hasn't had as good a day and night. I am so worried. (What Mr. Hunkins said.) I or we got letters from Aunt Mercy and Edith. And

I got one from Mr. Roberts and a very interesting paper. I laid down until 12 tonight and Aunt Laurinda stayed up and now I am up to stay with Mama. Irma went down to see the baby. Mert went down to the mill and up to the Mills.

Thursday, Feb. 21   How can I ever write in my diary again? Such a terrible day. The doctor came up this morning and said there was no hope. Mama was worse and has been vomiting all the morning. Dr. Russell went right back down town and sent for Dr. Madill. They came and performed an operation. Oh, such a terrible day. This is the second one like that I have been through. We sent for Mrs. Boyden to come and stay with us. She staid all night. I was nearly crazy. Poor dear Mama was so good and brave.

Friday, Feb. 22   Another terrible day. Words cannot express it— my precious mother laid and suffered all day. She was unconscious most all day and about 4 o'clock she was through with her terrible suffering and at rest with my dear father. I staid with her until the last—. Oh, it is too hard—. I can't stand it. Mert telephoned for Aunt Mercy and she came on the 4 o'clock train. Oh these terrible days, and now I am fatherless and motherless and I feel as if I were homeless. The dear old home all broken up and the dear father and mother together in heaven.

Saturday, Feb. 23   Aunt Mercy staid with me and the neighbors were in and out all day, but the terrible desolation. Mert telephoned to Edith and Mr. R. last night and heard from Edith today that she couldn't come. I lived through the day some way. I got letters from Edith and Mr. R. and some beautiful verses for Mama from Edith.[26] But my dear, dear mother will have to hear the verses from heaven. The neighbors called.

Sunday, Feb. 24   Another day dragged away and I lived on through all my trouble. The neighbors kept on coming and began to bring flowers. We got two telegrams from Mr. R. The first said he would come if possible. The last said he couldn't come so I have got to bear it without Edith and without him. Aunt Mercy staid with me.

Monday, Feb. 25   Another day went by and still the neighbors called and still I bore my trouble. I got beautiful letters from Edith and Mr. Roberts and a box of roses from Mr. R. Estace Earl came out and Uncle Ing and Aunt Nellie.[27]

Tuesday, Feb. 26   And now, today the friends and neighbors came and my precious mother surrounded by flowers was laid to rest beside my precious father. I arranged the flowers myself as I did before. I did it for both of them. Mr. Payson preached the most beautiful sermon I ever heard. We had the same bearers, the same music by the same singers, the same minister, the same kind of casket and the funeral at the same hours.[28]

Wednesday, Feb. 27   Lena[29] came home with me and staid all night. Estace staid until afternoon, then he started for home and took Lena with him and I am left alone with my sorrow. I got another letter from Edith and another from Mr. R., both fine. Irma went down and brought the baby home.

Thursday, Feb. 28   Pleasant. I began to straighten the house this morning and have worked hard all day sweeping, dusting and putting things in their places so tonight it looks like home again. We put up Mama's bed, Mert and I, and now Papa's and Mama's rooms are all fixed clean and nice but how it makes me feel. And yet it is a great comfort to look at those rooms.

MARCH

Friday, Mar. 1   I began the washing today, have worked at it all day and have got to leave part of it for tomorrow. It was hard work but I didn't mind that part of it.[30] I am so tired tonight and have no dear father and mother here to sympathize with me and feel sorry for me. Oh, it is so hard. It has been very windy today and has snowed some.

Saturday, Mar. 2   Very pleasant. I finished the washing, did up the work and had everything all slick by 3 o'clock. I read some and took a bath before I went to bed. Mert went to the village in the evening. I got two more beautiful letters, one from Edith and one from Mr. R. Mert got a fine one from Ed Ryder and one from Ada Lewis.

Sunday, Mar. 3   Very pleasant. I did up my work, got my dinner, and read some. Marvie and Fannie came between 1 & 2 o'clock and staid until about 4. I helped get dinner for them and finally about 5 o'clock went at my writing. The chimney burned out, the kitchen chimney. My, but we were frightened, and we worked for a while.[31] After the excitement I found my hand and wrist were burned. It was a terrible night.

Monday, Mar. 4   Real pleasant but windy. I did up my work then Willie Winslow and I went down town. He came up with Mert Saturday night. Mert started to carry him back last night but the weather was so terrible they couldn't go. This forenoon when he went down Mr. Case told him he didn't want him so he came back with me. I did quite a bit of running around down town. Called at Mr. Payson's to see him. Cora Pitt came along a little while after I got home and asked me to ride over to Mr. Endersbee's with her.[32]

Tuesday, Mar. 5   Pleasant, a real cold wind. Cora Pitt came along in the afternoon going to the village and I went with her. Had a good ride. I saw the Kahala girl in the waiting room. She talked so nice to me, and Mr. Austin and Mr. Lewis both spoke nicely to me. I have been doing a little of everything today, odd jobs.

Wednesday, Mar. 6   Pleasant, but cold. I have been ironing most all day besides doing up the work. I cooked down two batches of sauce juice into jelly. It is real good. The stage didn't bring our mail today. I am so sorry for I want it every time as soon as I expect it.

Thursday, Mar. 7   Our other chimney burned out this morning, and I had another scare. It was real cold in the morning but grew warmer, snowed hard in the afternoon. I got five fine letters, from Mr. Colson, Edith, Mr. Roberts, Aunt Mercy, and Mabel Lewis. I also got three papers from Mr. R. I ironed some more today.

Friday, Mar. 8   Warm and pleasant. I finished the ironing and made a pie and cake and swept and dusted my room. I also patched my underclothes and took a bath before I went to bed. I did quite a bit of work as I wanted to go to the village tomorrow.

Saturday, Mar. 9   Pleasant but quite warm. I drove down town, got down there about 12 o'clock. I did up all my work before I went and had the house as slick as could be. I did quite a lot of business, saw Mr. Hale,[33] sold two hams, got two "Plaindealers" etc. I went up to Lena's and she came home with me to stay until tomorrow afternoon. (I wish I could have a ride.) I got letters from Edith and Mr. R., also a paper from Mr. R.

Sunday, Mar. 10   Pleasant most all day but colder. Lena and I had a good visit last night and today. I carried her home toward night. Coming back, it rained all the way and the wind was very cold. I wore Mert's fur coat and three pairs of mittens. Now I am going to get my mail ready for tomorrow.

Monday, Mar. 11   It rained all day. Irma and the baby went down to her mother's. I gave the boys each a baked potato, a piece of pie and a piece of cake for their dinners. I worked on the scrapbook I am making, or receipt book rather. I sent four letters, a postal card and two papers this morning to be mailed.

Tuesday, Mar. 12   It snowed most all day. I did up my work and spent the rest of the time reading something I ought to know. Mr. Miller called to see about the marker and the inscription on the monument.[34] Zuar was here to see Mert in the evening but didn't come in to see me.

Wednesday, Mar. 13   Pleasant. I did up the work and worked on my receipt book again. Mert went to the village. I got letters from Edith, Mr. R. and Lena. Those two letters from away said just what I wanted them to say, and I thank God for them. I also got a paper from St. Louis.

Thursday, Mar. 14   Quite mild, snowed a little fine snow all day. Mrs. Pitt came down to see me in the afternoon and staid quite a while. I was glad to see her but how it made me think of Mama. I didn't do very much today but just do up my work and fuss around.

Friday, Mar. 15   Pleasant but colder. I did my housework and worked on my scrapbook in the afternoon. I had a headache and didn't feel well. Mert, Irma and Willie all went up to the Foresters' supper. They were gone seven hours and I was left alone. I was sick and nervous and couldn't go to sleep for a long time. Such a time as I had.

Saturday, Mar. 16   Very pleasant. I didn't feel well all day. Mrs. Boyden came down to see me in the afternoon. I was glad to see her. She talked nice to me. I got a letter from Mr. Roberts, two letters from Edith, and a picture of Carroll's and Kathleen's Christmas tree and a paper from Mr. R.

Sunday, Mar. 17   Quite mild, snowed most all day. I did up the work and wrote two letters, then got dinner. Just after I had eaten my dinner Zuar came and staid until 3:30. I was glad he came. After he went away I wrote another letter.

Monday, Mar. 18   Very pleasant. I got up, got my breakfast and washed the dishes, swept and fed the hens, but I was sick, and after I got that much done I had to undress and go to bed. About noon a man came to see me, tax collector, and I had to get up. Then I staid up and fixed my old black waist to wear and ripped up another old waist.

Tuesday, Mar. 19   Quite pleasant, but very cold wind. I could hardly get warm all day. I made some cookies just as I was a mind to see how they would turn out. They were just fine. I gave them ½ doz. out in the other part and they thought them very nice and wanted the receipt. I filled and washed all my lamps.[35] Mert went to the village in the evening.

Wednesday, Mar. 20   Pleasant. When I got up, I found the mail. Mert got it last night. I got letters from Mr. Roberts, Edith, and Aunt Mercy. It staid pleasant until toward night, then clouded up and began to rain. It rained hard in the evening. I wrote long letters to Edith and Mr. Roberts.

Thursday, Mar. 21   Quite pleasant. This morning, the brook was all overflowed. It must have rained all night last night. I did my work, washed out my underclothes, and made some biscuits extra. Grace Boyden came down to see me in the afternoon and staid to supper. Mert called me to come out and hear the baby talk to Willie today.

Friday, Mar. 22   Pleasant in the morning, but began to snow toward noon and stormed most of the rest of the day, regular March weather. I swept and dusted my room. Mert went to the village and got the mail. I got a letter from Mr. R. that did me lots of good. I also got a St. Louis paper and "The Universalist Leader."[36]

Saturday, Mar. 23   Very pleasant and quite warm. I swept and dusted the sitting room and bedrooms. Made a ginger cake and started some bread. I took a bath in the afternoon and read some in the evening. The stage didn't bring the mail and I was disappointed. Gene was up to see Mert in the evening, but I didn't see him.

Sunday, Mar. 24   It rained a little most all day, cleared off toward night. I wrote my letter in the forenoon and read in the afternoon. I was so lonesome. Mert, Irma, and the baby went down to Mr. Carter's to dinner. Mert came back and Willie went away. Zuar came down and spent the evening with me. I was glad to see him for I was lonesome.

Monday, Mar. 25   Very pleasant. I washed, got it all done before dinner. Mert went away in the forenoon. I sent for the mail and got Edith's Saturday letter, I mean the one I ought to have had Saturday, and my

"Ladies' Home Journal" for April and my St. Louis paper and the Potsdam paper. I read in the evening and some in the afternoon.

Tuesday, Mar. 26   Pleasant in the morning but it began to rain in the afternoon. Grew worse until it was raining hard in the evening. I started to go to Canton. The roads are something awful, neither sleighing or wheeling.[37] I got down to Little River nearly and the water was over the road so I could go no further.[38] I had the cutter. Mert took the buggy and went down to Lodge. Dora Taylor called here in the forenoon.[39]

Wednesday, Mar. 27   It stormed all day, either rain or snow. Mert came home about 9:30. I got a letter from Edith. Last night was an awful night. Mert had to stay down until morning. The river is awful. Yesterday, 5 people got in trying to cross it but they were all saved. Mr. R.'s letter didn't come and I am so lonesome without it. I wrote a long letter to Edith. I did quite a lot of mending. I felt so sorry for my poor brother today. Mert went over to Boyden's sugar house and got a pail of syrup.[40]

Thursday, Mar. 28   Snowed all day. I did some mending. The stage brought the mail. I got a paper from St. Louis and a present from Mr. Milburn that I think a great deal of. I didn't get any letter from Mr. Roberts though. I am wondering what the matter is. I am so sorry his letter didn't come.

Friday, Mar. 29   Quite cold and snowed some. Mert and Willie went to the village. I got my letter from Mr. R. and a fine one from Mr. Milburn. They both came to Canton Wednesday so I don't see why I didn't get them yesterday. Mert, Irma, and Willie all went up to a sugar social (Foresters). I hated to stay alone so I went up and asked Cora to come and stay with me. She came and we had a good visit. I wiped the dishes for Mrs. Pitt while Cora was getting ready. It was a nice moonlight night.

Saturday, Mar. 30   Very pleasant. Cora staid quite a little while after breakfast, then went home. I did the work all up and had the house all slick. I got a letter from Edith and one from Mr. Roberts. Mert and I had a scene this morning.[41] I am most crazy for I don't know what to do or what is right for me to do. I took my "Universalist Leader" up stairs and read it through to see if I could find something to help me and I did. How I wish I knew what to do.

Sunday, Mar. 31   Snowed most all day but was bright moonlight in the evening. I wrote my letters in the forenoon and read in the afternoon. Zuar came down about 7 o'clock in the evening and staid until 'most 1. We had a talk that made me feel just like crying but he was <u>very</u> kind to me. No one could have been better. I wish there wasn't so much on my mind. I am nearly crazy, so much all at once and all kinds of things. I wish someone could help me.

APRIL

Monday, April 1   Snowed hard in the forenoon but cleared off in the afternoon and grew warmer. I drove down town, rode in an awful storm all the way down and got cold but it was much warmer coming back. I got my St. Louis paper. I got the check cashed and paid some of the small debts. Such a time as I had getting past the track coming home. There was a freight train right by the road and Fred[42] wouldn't go past it.

Tuesday, April 2   A beautiful day. After I got my work done, I worked on my sofa pillow. Mert came back. Irma went down for him. I got a postal from Aunt Mercy and a letter from Estace. Em is real sick.

Wednesday, April 3   A very stormy day. It rained hard until late in the afternoon, then it turned to snow. Stormed hard all day long and at night the wind blew a hurricane. I wrote five letters and worked on my sofa pillow besides doing up my work. The stage didn't bring the mail today, I suppose on account of the weather. I was disappointed.

Thursday, April 4   It rained in the forenoon and was misty, cleared off in the afternoon. Mr. Pitt stopped and told me they were going to sugar off and it would be ready about 2 o'clock.[43] I couldn't go for I had to watch for the stage. I got letters from Edith and Mr. Roberts. I worked on my worsted crazy sofa pillow.

Friday, April 5   Kind of foggy but quite nice out. Dolph called to see me in the forenoon and talked very nicely to me. I finished my worsted work. In the afternoon I went up to Mr. Pitt's, staid until most night and ate a lot of warm sugar. Then I called over to Mr. Boyden's, got some syrup and some sweet apples to bring home. Mrs. Boyden told me about Zuar going away! Oh, I am so sorry. What can I do? I feel as if there was nothing right in my life at all.

Saturday, April 6   Cloudy most all day. I did my work. How I did feel all day. I don't believe anything will ever come right in my life again. It is too hard to have so much trouble at once. I got letters from Edith, Mr. R. and Larnard. How I would have liked to have got just one more letter.

Sunday, April 7   It rained all day, was rainy, muddy and disagreeable. I wrote letters and cried most all day. Oh, it seems if I would go wild. They all went down to Mr. Carter's and I was alone but it doesn't matter.

Monday, April 8   It snowed hard in the morning but turned to rain and kept it up all day. I drove up to the Mills to send the mail as I had a package that had to be weighed. The roads and weather were something awful, and I got cold and wet. Had quite a time getting through the teams at the factory. I just kind of fussed around the rest of the day after getting dinner and doing up my work.

Tuesday, April 9   Rained all day long. Such weather! I fixed two of my dress skirts and worked some in my scrapbook of recipes. Mert and Willie went over to Boyden's sugar house and heard that Zuar's folks had heard from him and that he is in Vermont. I am so glad that they have heard from him. One of the cows got in the spring.

Wednesday, April 10   It didn't rain or snow, was quite a nice day although the sun didn't shine much. The stage didn't bring the mail. I was sorry. I did my work, kept busy the most of the time. I laid down a few minutes in the afternoon. The chimney burned out again, or started to, the one in Mert's part.

Thursday, April 11   Real pleasant. I worked on some crazy work after my housework was done. Willie went to the village and got the mail. I got a letter from Edith and one from Lena. We got one from Norwood saying Em was dead and one from Aunt Susan. I walked up to Mr. Pitt's to borrow Cora's jacket to wear to the funeral tomorrow. I called over to Mr. Boyden's and took their jar and basket home. I had a hard headache.

Friday, April 12   A beautiful day, warm and bright. I didn't sleep much last night. I had such awful pains all through my head and face. Mert and I drove to Canton and took the noon train for Norwood. Ten went on that train over to Em's funeral. There was a large funeral. Mert came back on the 3:25 train. I staid all night and went up to Will's to sleep as the beds were all full at Ed's. My head and face still pain me.

Saturday, April 13   Very warm and pleasant. I staid at Will's until about 10 o'clock then went over to Ed's. I didn't feel well at all. I came home on the 3:25 train today. Net and Ethel came too. They staid last night. Willie was down after me, such a time as I had with that pain. I was sick at night but slept pretty good. I got a letter from Mr. Roberts and one from Mabel Lewis. I have got something else to worry about now. This is Mert's birthday.

Sunday, April 14   Very pleasant. I did up my work and wrote my letters. Ella and Grace Boyden came down to call on me and staid quite a little while. Toward night I walked up to Mr. Pitt's and carried Cora's jacket home. Blanche Randall was there so I had a little visit with her. Cora and Blanche came a piece with me.

Monday, April 15   Very pleasant. I did up my work and did some extra work. In the afternoon Blanche came down and staid a little while, then I went back with her up to Mr. Pitt's to eat warm sugar and I also staid to supper. Got home just at dark. My head and face pained me badly today.

Tuesday, April 16   Very pleasant. I did my work and worked quite a little on my crazy work. I also looked over the boxes in the cupboard in the big room. Mert went to the village and got the mail but I didn't get any letters. I went for a walk toward night and staid out until dark. I enjoyed it so much.

Wednesday, April 17   Very pleasant. I did my common work and fussed around doing whatever I wanted to. The stage brought the mail. I got letters from Edith and Mr. R. I answered their letters and cried, I felt so lonely and desolate. I went for a walk after supper and sat on a rock in the pasture until dark. It was lovely. I went to the woods in the forenoon and got quite a lot of mayflowers and sat on a log for quite a while.

Thursday, April 18   Cloudy but quite warm. The stage didn't come this way, so I couldn't send my letters. The boys went fishing last night. Mert gave me two of the fish. About noon, Marvie, Fannie, Leona, and Harold came. They ate dinner in Mert's part and supper with me and staid all night. The boys went fishing in the afternoon and caught 26 nice large fish.

Friday, April 19   Rained most all day. They ate breakfast with me this morning and dinner with Mert and went to Uncle Nelson's in the afternoon. I sent my letters this morning. Mert and Marvie went to the village but Mert didn't get the mail. I worked some on my crazy work.

Saturday, April 20   Cold and windy. The chimney burned out again, awful hard. I was frightened. Marvie's folks came along here on their way home and stopped a while. The stage didn't bring the mail and I was so disappointed. It began to rain toward night. I walked down to the mailbox to see if he left the mail there and got soaking wet. I haven't had much fire today.

Sunday, April 21   The sun shone a few minutes in the morning, but it was cloudy most all day and rained some, quite hard toward night. I did up my work, took a bath, read some, wrote three letters and copied my poem for Larnard.

Monday, April 22   Very pleasant but windy until just at night, when it rained very hard. I did quite a washing and brought and emptied all the water myself. Got kind of tired. Mert went to the village. Irma and the baby went down to Mr. Carter's I suppose. I got letters from Edith and Mr. Roberts. His letter made me feel better.

Tuesday, April 23   Cloudy and rainy. I did my work, baked bread and looked over the bureau drawers in my room and some old letters. I got so tired and my back ached so I laid down toward night and Mama's and my little stripped cat laid down with me.

Wednesday, April 24   Pleasant. I did the work up, did a little mending etc. I did some ironing too. The stage brought the mail. I got letters from Edith and Mr. R. again. I also got papers from St. Louis Monday and today.

Thursday, April 25   Pleasant but the wind blew very hard. I fussed around doing a little of everything up stairs and down cellar. I held the baby quite a while in the afternoon while her mother was hanging up clothes. I sat in the parlor in the sunshine in the afternoon. It was warm and pleasant in there. This is Papa's birthday and I wanted to go to the woods, get some flowers and take them down to the cemetary but the wind blew so I gave it up.

Friday, April 26   Pleasant and windy again. I thought of going up to Mr. Boyden's today but gave it up. I did whatever I thought of today too. Just at night I went for a walk and walked up to Mr. Pitt's, came back by moonlight. Heard Anson had got home.

Saturday, April 27   Very pleasant and warm. I did the Saturday's work.[44] Made the house look as neat and nice as could be. I took my bath in the afternoon. Mert went to the village. I got a letter from Edith but none from Mr. R. Wonder why I didn't get his. Toward night I drove up to the Mills, sold my eggs and got some groceries, stopped to see Mr. Barrows about the insurance. Drove up and paid Mr. Cleflin and Mr. Wallace.

Sunday, April 28   Very pleasant and warm. I did up the work, didn't have anything else to do but get breakfast, wash dishes and make my bed. Then I changed my waist and wrote to Edith and Mr. Roberts. I read some and sat out on the porch a long time both in the sunlight and moonlight. There was a June bug flying around. Curly[45] and the little cat sat on the porch with me. I just had fire enough to get breakfast and haven't had any since. How I wanted a certain young man today.

Monday, April 29   Very pleasant and warm. Mert and I went to the village. I had a good ride. Got my new hat, shoes, and sateen waist. I got a good letter from Mr. Roberts. Mrs. Kilbourn talked nicely to me. I sat out on the porch a long time tonight. It was fine. Mert says Zuar is around here somewhere.

Tuesday, April 30   It rained nearly all day. I was so lonely. I had a fire today and got warm meals and boiled part of a ham and cooked up a jar of sauce that was worked and some jelly that was worked and baked some apples. I starched and ironed my white shirtwaist. I laid down in the afternoon. Mr. Nickerson brought the flowers Mama ordered for the cemetary. I ate an orange and banana.

MAY

Wednesday, May 1   Very pleasant. I drove over to Mr. Drury's to ask him to set out the plants in the cemetery. I staid to dinner and Mr. Drury came over with me and set out the weeping willow and rose bushes. I called at Lee Wallace's to get a pail of water for the plants.[46] After I got home I went to the woods and got a basket full and hand full of beautiful flowers, found beds and beds of the bloodroot blossoms, such lovely fragrant pure white ones. I have four beautiful bouquets. I didn't get my mail today. Mert and Willie went down town in the evening.

Thursday, May 2   We had a thunder shower in the morning. It rained hard all the forenoon but not as much in the afternoon. I wrote to Edith and Mr. R. Just at night I walked down to the corner and looked in the mailbox and found mail there. I got letters from Edith and Mr. R. and they did me so much good. I also got two papers from St. Louis and the "Plaindealer." I finished sewing the lace on the handkerchief Mama hemmed and sent it to Edith.

Friday, May 3   Pleasant but a very cold wind. I went down to the corner to send a letter to Mr. R. by the stage, was early so called at Mrs. Bluett's.[47] Pearl and Rob came up home with me to get a paper off Mert. I did just what I wanted to the rest of the day.

Saturday, May 4   Very pleasant. I went down to the cemetary in the morning, took my bouquets and the last two scarlet lilies, and went cross lots through the woods and got some more flowers. I staid quite a while by my father's and mother's graves.[48] I did my Saturday's work when I got back and took my bath toward night and changed my clothes. The stage brought the mail. I got two fine letters from Edith and Mr. R.

Sunday, May 5   Very pleasant, just a fine day. I wrote my letters and got my mail all ready to send tomorrow morning. Toward night I walked up to Mr. Pitt's to get their "Plaindealer." Mrs. Croft was there. I went out and got the baby this morning when she was crying and kept her quite a while. She went to sleep after a while. Anson called just at night. Oh dear, I just don't know what to do. Willie brought Mabel Hunt down here. They staid to supper in Mert's part.

Monday, May 6   Very pleasant and warm. I walked down to the corner with my letters in the morning. Worked on my crazy work in the afternoon. I just spent a lonesome day, thought some of going to the village with Mr. Pitt, but didn't.

Tuesday, May 7   Very pleasant and warm. I started to walk to Canton or catch a ride, but Mr. Bluett let me take his horse and buggy. I staid down until night. Such a time as I had with a hat. I called up to Mr. Gardner's and brought home two books to read. I had a great time bringing up all my bundles from Mr. Bluett's. I heard that Uncle Allen is dead.

Wednesday, May 8   Very warm and pleasant. In the morning, I walked down to the corner to see the stage and called up to Carrie and Mame Bullis to see if they had any flowers.[49] When I came home I got ready and walked up to Mr. Boyden's to see if I could ride up to Mr. Langdon's funeral with them. I rode. When I got back I walked down to the corner after the mail, and Jim Lindley came along and I rode home with him.[50] Walter Andrews went by and laughed to see me riding with him. I got letters from Edith and Mr. Roberts.

Thursday, May 9   Pleasant and a little cooler. We started about 9 o'clock for Norwood. Had a lovely ride. I felt sick in the morning. We staid until toward night until it was cooler before starting for home. Edie B. came home with us. We drove around by the paper mill and called at Will's and Marvie's. In the afternoon Edie and I went for a walk over to the post office and we girls all went for a walk up the bank to see the new railroad. Saw Mr. Bonham. We went up to Mrs. Adams window to see Harry the parrot. Uncle Allen looked natural. I got the dozen carnations that Edith ordered for the cemetary.

Friday, May 10   Warm and pleasant until afternoon when a big shower came up. It just poured and thundered and lightened. Edie and I went down to the cemetary with the beautiful carnations after the rain. We rode down with Mert and walked back. We played games in the evening. Willie came in and played with us. We wanted to go to Canton in the evening but the weather and roads prevented it.

Saturday, May 11   Rainy. We couldn't get to town today, either. I got letters from Edith and Mr. Roberts, fine ones as usual. I worked most all day, doing the Saturday's work and some baking. Willie, Mert, and Irma all came in and played games with Edie and I in the evening. We didn't go to bed until 11 o'clock either tonight or last night.

Sunday, May 12   Pleasant most all day. Edith played on the organ most all day. I read a little but not much. Willie was in here the most of the afternoon and evening. Willie, Edie and I started to go up to the Mills to church but the wind blew so and it began to rain so we turned around and came home. They all came in here to hear Edie play in the evening. Tom Carter and some young lady were here to see Irma.

Monday, May 13   Very cold and windy and rainy. I carried Edie over to Net's.[51] I staid to dinner and supper both. We were most frozen when we got there, it was so cold. I had the worst luck trying to mail my letters and then didn't get them mailed. Net and I had quite a talk. We had a big storm right after supper.

Tuesday, May 14   Pleasant and warmer. I went to bed early last night and didn't get up until between 8 and 9 this morning so had a good sleep. Mert went to the village and took my letters to mail. I fussed around. Went for a walk just at night. I am so lonesome.

Wednesday, May 15   Very pleasant. I worked some on a sofa pillow. Uncle Ing came a little after noon, staid until about 3:30. Then went up to Uncle Nelson's. Jim Lindley came with the grocery cart. I sold him my eggs and bought two lemons. I went down after the mail, got the letters from Edith and Mr. R., fine ones as usual. Got a very interesting paper from St. Louis and the "Plaindealer," Malone paper, Potsdam paper and "Universalist Leader."

Thursday, May 16   Very pleasant. I went down to the corner to mail my letters, sat on the side of the road a long time waiting for the stage. I did up my work and then worked in my flower garden. I got most awful tired. I laid down toward night and slept a while then worked in my garden until dark. Then ate supper and read a while in "Eben Holden"[52] before going to bed.

Friday, May 17   Cloudy all day so it was a better day to work in my flower garden. I finished putting in the seeds and set out the plants. In the forenoon I made some cookies and brown bread. I laid down again in the afternoon toward night and read before going to bed.

Saturday, May 18   Rained nearly all the time all day. I slicked things up, up stairs and down. Did quite a big day's work. Made a cake, cooked some beans and boiled some ham so I will have something to eat over Sunday. I got letters from Edith, Mr. Roberts and Larnard. Took a bath toward night and read some more before going to bed. I sat in the parlor for quite a while thinking just at twilight.

Sunday, May 19   It rained nearly all day. I wrote my letters and read some. I was lonesome. Anson drove in and talked with Mert quite a little while but didn't come in. I finished reading "Eben Holden" and started "To Have and To Hold."[53]

Monday, May 20   Cloudy. I got ready and rode to Canton with Mr. Pitt. We had a great talk. I saw Mr. Payson and gave him $5.00. Got a St. Louis paper. Got my white waist at Mrs. Griffith's. I like it real well since it is fixed. Left the insertion Mama made for her to put into a skirt for me. Brought home two shirt waists from Whitmarsh's to try on.

Tuesday, May 21   Very pleasant. I did quite a big washing and cleaned off the table down cellar and arranged the jars. I was tired. I walked up the road just at night. Curly and the little stripped cat went with me. Pearl Bluett came along, going up to Mr. Pitt's. She stopped a little while when she came back. I went a little piece with her. Mert and Willie went to the village in the evening.

Wednesday, May 22   Very warm and sultry until late in the afternoon, when it began to rain. I sat out in the yard to do my mending and tried to keep cool. Maud and I sat out on the steps a while. I got letters from Edith and Mr. Roberts. His made me feel very sad. I answered their letters.

Thursday, May 23   Real pleasant but windy. I ironed some, did my common work and read some. The boys and Curly went fishing. Curly brought a mud turtle home with him. I walked down to the corner to mail my letters in the morning, rode back with Willie from the factory.[54]

Friday, May 24   Rained hard for quite a while most of the forenoon. Was cloudy all day. Mert came in and talked to me. He talked nice about settling things. Willie went up to the Mills and talked with Ed Rider through the telephone. He is going to Malone tomorrow, has a job there. The wind blew a hurricane all day.

Saturday, May 25   Real pleasant the most of the time except an awful wind, but it rained in the morning and was cold. I slicked up the house, took my bath in the afternoon and walked down to the corner for the mail. I got letters from Edith, Mr. R. and Aunt Laurinda. Got my "Ladies' Home Journal." Mert carried Willie down to take the train. He got about half the mail and the stage driver the other half. I went for a walk toward night up to the hill and sat on a big rock for quite a while.

Sunday, May 26   A beautiful day until just at night, it sprinkled a little. I wrote three letters, took me a good share of the day. I finished reading "To Have and To Hold." Mert, Irma and the baby went down to Mr. Carter's, so I was left alone. I was so lonesome tonight. I sat out on the porch quite a while just at dusk and felt almost as if I hadn't a friend in the world.

Monday, May 27   Cloudy and rained a little in the forenoon but cleared off and was real nice after that and very warm. I drove down town. The roads are awful. I went up to Mr. Gardner's to dinner. Lena and I went down street after dinner. We went in and got some soda water. (In the post office.) I paid Mr. Leighton and Mr. Barnes what we owed them.

Tuesday, May 28　　　　Cloudy and cool most all day. I sewed some after doing my housework. Mert went over to Mike Peter's wife's funeral. I laid down a while in the afternoon. Went to bed before it was dark enough to light a lamp.

Wednesday, May 29　　　　Cloudy most of the time. The sun shone out once in a while. It rained a little in the afternoon. I got letters telling me what the Drs. charges are. Got a letter from Edith. Didn't get any letters from Mr. R. but got a paper and a box of beautiful flowers, 14 roses, red, pink, yellow and white, 14 carnations, red, pink and white, some sweet peas and some ferns. Now I have got some flowers for my precious father and mother if it is so wet I can't go to pick them.

Thursday, May 30　　　　Rained part of the time and was pleasant part of the time. In the morning, I started to walk down to the corner with six letters, but Milton Pitt came along going to town and took them. A little before noon I took my flowers and walked down to the cemetary. The grass was very wet so I couldn't sit down or stay long. I stopped and talked with Mrs. Bluett and the children a few minutes. After supper I walked up to Mr. Pitt's and staid until most dark. Mrs. Pitt wasn't very well.

Friday, May 31　　　　Rained most all day. Mert went to the woods and made me a pretty rustic stand. It was kind of him. I didn't know anything about it until I saw him bringing it. I looked over some things up stairs and swept up there and washed the woodwork in the sitting room. I was tired and laid down a while in the afternoon. Guy Poole came today to work for Mert.

JUNE

Saturday, June 1　　　　Pleasant part of the time and rained part of the time as usual. I did my Saturday work and took my bath, then read a while. I was waiting for the mail. I got letters from Edith, Mr. Roberts and one from Dr. Madill. Got a box of lilies of the valley from Edith. Mert, Irma and baby went away. When they came back I brought the baby in here for a while until it warmed up out there.

Sunday, June 2   Pleasant until toward night, then it rained and just before dark thundered and lightened. I wrote nearly all day. Long letters to Edith and Mr. R. Thirty-five pages in one and about thirty in the other one. I was very lonely. If it hadn't been for my writing I don't know what I would have done.

Monday, June 3   Rained about all day, just poured part of the time. I sent my letters by Mr. Pitt. I worked on my crazy work. Mert and Guy went to the village. Guy got a new buggy. Irma and I went over to see it after supper. I made soup for supper for all.

Tuesday, June 4   Very pleasant. I did up my work, mended a shirtwaist, then got ready and went up to Mr. Boyden's. Grandma was all alone and she and I had a good visit. She got dinner for us. Mrs. McClellan came over there in the afternoon and Mr. Elmer came a little while before I came away. I came along to Mr. Pitt's and staid there until about dark. Mrs. Langdon was there. They all talked to me and kept my mind off my trouble a good deal for one day.

Wednesday, June 5   Very pleasant. I felt sick in the forenoon and took a hot drink and laid down for a while then got up and walked down to the cemetary with Edith's lilies of the valley. I called at Anne Wallace's and at the Misses Rodee's. Felt so sick walking home I could hardly walk. I got letters from Edith, Aunt Mercy and Mr. Hale. I am wondering why Mr. Roberts letter didn't come.

Thursday, June 6   Pleasant in the morning but windy. In fact it was so until toward night, when it rained a little and cleared off again. I walked down with my mail to the corner and walked down again at night. It was very warm. I worked on my crazy work. Irma came in and sat quite a while just at night.

Friday, June 7   Rained, stopped in the afternoon. Mert went to the village in the afternoon. I made a cake out of all I wanted to get rid of. It was pretty good. I did my work and worked on my crazy work.

Saturday, June 8   It rained showers all day. I went to the village in the afternoon, drove my own horse, such roads and such a shower, but I reached town all right. Got two letters from Mr. Roberts and the Sunday paper, and a picture and a letter from Edith. Paid Dr. Wilson $10. Saw Anson. Came back round by Langdon's Corners. The roads are much better that way. Drove up to see Mr. Barrows about the insurance. Had pretty good luck today after all.

Sunday, June 9   Cold and windy, I was alone a good share of the day. I read quite a bit and wrote three letters. I was so lonesome, how I wished someone would come to see me but no one came. I sat out on the porch at night and walked around some. No, I didn't sit on the porch, I sat in the parlor.

Monday, June 10   Very pleasant. I walked down to mail my letters and called at Mrs. Bluett's and waited a long time for the stage, but it didn't come so must have gone some other road. In the afternoon Mert and Irma went out to Hewittsville. I got supper for Guy, he went somewhere after supper for a little while and I rode with him up to Mr. Pitt's and staid all night with Cora. Guy mailed my letters up to the Mills.

Tuesday, June 11   Very pleasant. I got up early and came home to get breakfast for Guy. I also got dinner and supper. We had a great talk. He went away after supper and I was left alone. Curly and the two cats went for a walk with me up and down the road. Mert and Irma got home about 10 o'clock.

Wednesday, June 12   Very pleasant and warm. I walked up to Mr. Pitt's and staid to dinner. Talked with Mr. and Mrs. Pitt about settling affairs. Hoed out my flower garden in the morning. The stage didn't bring the mail but the boys drove down for it in the evening. I talked with Mert about the price of the farm etc. He talked real good but we both got cross before we got through and said things I am sorry for. Mert cried once and it made me feel so bad. I must be an awful cross queer thing.

Thursday, June 13   Pleasant and warm, very warm. I walked down to mail my letters and waited at Mrs. Bluett's, when I came back I did up my work. Washed up and dressed as cool as I could and did some writing. In the afternoon I took the baby for a ride and we called on Mrs. Pitt. The baby is an awful cute little dud and isn't afraid of anyone. I wrote some more and went to bed early. The mail was here on the table when I got up. I got letters from Edith and Mr. R. and Larnard, all fine letters, a St. Louis Sunday paper and picture.

Friday, June 14   Pleasant and very warm. I walked down to the cemetary with a basket of flowers, some roses and lilies from our front yard and some pansies and honeysuckle I got at Mrs. Pitt's. Papa's and Mama's headstones are up and look nice. The rose bushes and weeping willow are doing nicely. I called at Anna Wallace's and rested and cooled off. I had the baby in here a little while sitting up in the rocking chair in the afternoon. The wind breezed up toward night and it turned cooler.

Saturday, June 15   Much cooler. I swept and dusted up stairs and down and slicked up. Took my bath in the afternoon and walked down to the corner for the mail. Got letters from Edith and Mr. R., a St. Louis paper and the Potsdam paper and "Universalist Leader." The boys went to the village in the afternoon. I went to bed early.

Sunday, June 16   Very pleasant. How I wanted to go for a ride but couldn't. I wrote all the afternoon. I picked bouquets and trimmed up the house with them. It looked nice. I wished that someone would come see me or that I could go somewhere for I was so lonely.

Monday, June 17   Very pleasant. I did up my work and got ready to go to town if I got the chance. I rode with Mr. Pitt and Miltie. Walked up to Mr. Bailey's and got the buildings insured. They were all very pleasant to me. Did some trading for Irma. I rode home with Mrs. Gibson. Had a good ride and a good talk. She came this way on my account.

Tuesday, June 18   Cloudy mostly and rained some. I did up my work and picked up the vegetables out of the cellar, cooked what was good of them and threw the rest away. I worked in my flower garden some in the afternoon.

Wednesday, June 19   Very warm and pleasant in the forenoon. Clouded up and thundered and rained in the afternoon then cleared off again. I wrote letters most all day. The stage brought the mail right here today. I got letters from Edith and Mr. R. and the St. Louis paper and picture.

Thursday, June 20   I did up my work then drove up to the Mills, mailed my letters and left word to Mr. Barrows not to hand my name into the Grange. I drove Guy's new buggy. It clouded up some after I got home and rained very hard. I worked on Mama's carpet rags.[55] Mert made a scarecrow for the cornfield.

Friday, June 21   Pleasant. I did my washing and my Saturday's work. Was very tired and went to bed at 7:30. Mert went to the village. I read some just at night.

Saturday, June 22   Pleasant and very warm. Thundered toward night. I did my ironing in the forenoon. Read a while and took my bath in the afternoon. Walked down to the corner for the mail. Got a letter from Edith.

Sunday, June 23   Pleasant until toward night when it rained a little while. Oh, I was so lonesome. I read quite a lot and wrote to Edith. I was alone for quite a while. The baby went to church. It was children's day at Brick Chapel.

Monday, June 24   Very warm. I walked down to the corner twice to get the mail and send my letters. I did my work and my mending. Got a letter and paper from Mr. R. and the insurance policy from Ogdensburg. I answered Mr. R.'s letter. We all went out and picked strawberries for a shortcake. I helped look them over and Irma made the shortcake and cut it in four pieces.

Tuesday, June 25   Pleasant and very warm. I walked down to the corner to mail a letter and called up to Mrs. Bluett's a while waiting for the stage. I did up my work and worked on Mama's carpet rags. I laid down on the parlor floor in the afternoon to rest. A load of college students[56] were out for a ride and one of the young gentlemen stopped to ask where Waterman Hill was and about the road to Canton this way.

Wednesday, June 26   Pleasant and very warm again. I did up my work and then worked on the carpet rags again. Grace Boyden came down to spend the afternoon with me and staid to supper. I got a letter from Mr. Roberts, the "Plaindealer," and the "Ladies' Home Journal." I am so anxious because Edith's letter didn't come. They all went to the ice cream social at Brick Chapel, and I was left alone.

Thursday, June 27   Very pleasant and warm. I went to town, mailed my letters and paid Dr. McKay, then went up to Lena's to dinner. Staid all the afternoon and to supper. Then Lena and I went down street and I did some trading and started for home. Lena rode up to the bridge with me. When I got home, Aunt Mercy was here. She and I had a good visit. Didn't get to bed until 12. I got Edith's letter. I was so glad.

Friday, June 28   Warm and pleasant again. Aunt Mercy went home about 8:30. I wanted her to stay longer. I felt so lonesome after she had gone. Mert went to the village in the forenoon. I didn't do much but read besides the housework that I had to do.

Saturday, June 29   Warm and pleasant. I cleaned up down cellar and did up my Saturday's work. In the evening Mert, Irma and I went up to the Mills to the Pawnee Indian entertainment. Mert asked me to go in the afternoon. I enjoyed the ride and getting out among people. The stage didn't bring the mail. I was so disappointed. Will Thompson drove over here, had been to Aunt Laurinda's.

Sunday, June 30   Pleasant and cooler. I did up my work, was a little late getting up, and walked down to Mr. Bluett's to see if he got the mail last night. He said he would but changed his mind and didn't go, so I haven't my mail yet. I laid down a while in the afternoon and then wrote some letters.

JULY

Monday, July 1   Cloudy in the morning and rained a little. Mert went to the village. He took my letters down to the corner to mail them but didn't see the stage so came back and took them to Canton. He was going in the afternoon. It came off pleasant in the afternoon. The boys began haying today. I went out to work in my flower garden after supper. Mert didn't feel very well and I was so afraid he was going to be sick. Mr. Cole and his two girls called just at night. Mert got the mail. I got a letter from Edith but none from Mr. R.

Tuesday, July 2   Pleasant and a little cooler in the morning, but warm as ever in the afternoon. I woke up and felt sick, dressed and went down stairs and laid down on the lounge. Didn't build any fire or get any breakfast. About noon I got up and got a meal and ate. It was breakfast and dinner together. I sewed on some carpet rags in the afternoon and read some. Worked in my flower garden in the evening.

Wednesday, July 3   Pleasant and a little cooler. Mr. Frazer from Prescott[57] called this morning about 7 o'clock, came over with Uncle Nelson. Made a short call but a pleasant one. I made a loaf of bread and a fine cake, a small one. In the afternoon I walked down to see if the stage brought the mail but found the box empty. Called at Mrs. Bluett's. Then walked up to Mr. Pitt's, staid to supper, got some lovely flowers, some lettuce, and the rustic work Milton made for me to bring home.

Thursday, July 4   Rained a little once in a while. I walked down to the corner with my letters in the morning and called on Mrs. Poole at the factory.[58] The boys went to the village last night and I sat up to get my letters. They got home at about 11. I read my letters and answered them, went to bed between 1 and 2 o'clock. Got letters from Edith and Mr. R. and my St. Louis paper and picture. I wrote to Aunt Mercy and Larnard. Laid down in the forenoon and slept for a while. Irma asked me to eat dinner out there.

Friday, July 5   Cloudy most of the time. Rained a little bit. Mert and Irma went to the village. After dinner I walked down to the cemetary with some flowers. I called at Lee Wallace's, got to talking and staid quite a while. One of the rose bushes at the cemetary has quite a lot of buds on it. When I got back I worked in my flower garden until dark. Got a fine letter from Mabel Lewis. (Jim Lindley's card.)

Saturday, July 6   Pleasant. It rained quite hard in the night last night and thundered and lightened some. I woke up for a few minutes but went to sleep again. I did my Saturday's work in the forenoon and went to the village in the afternoon. Came home the other way and then cut across by Mr. Squires on that cross road. Had a good visit with Mrs. Griffith. Got fine letters from Mr. R. and Edith and a paper, the St. Louis paper.

Sunday, July 7   Pleasant mostly, a few showers. I read quite a bit and wrote my letters. I was very lonesome as usual.

Monday, July 8   Pleasant. I walked down to the corner to mail my letters, just missed the stage. Walked up to Mr. Bluett's and he sent them for me by Mr. Bird. Mr. Hemenway and Elsworth Poole came along here and stopped with a sick horse. The horse and Mr. Hemenway were here quite a while. Mr. Poole took Fred horse and drove to Canton. Maggy Boyden and Nora called in the afternoon. I worked in my flower garden after supper.

Tuesday, July 9   Pleasant and warmer again. I got up at 4 o'clock. Did my common work, my washing, washed the sitting room windows etc. Did quite a bit and was tired. Got most of my work done in the forenoon and took a bath and laid down in the afternoon. Brought the baby in here after supper and held her a long while. Read some in the evening.

Wednesday, July 10   Pleasant. I did my common work and made some cookies and washed the lamps extra. Mert went to the village. I got letters from Edith and Mr. R. Mert got part of the mail and I walked down to the corner and got the rest. Aunt Mercy and Edie B. drove in in the forenoon, were going up to Mr. Mott's and coming back here to stay all night. Aunt Mercy and Edie came back. Edie played and sang most all the evening. Mert, Irma and the baby were all in here.

Thursday, July 11   Pleasant. Aunt Mercy and Edie started home about 10. I did up my work and read some. I was so lonesome but then I am always lonesome now and probably always will be. We planned it for me to go down to Norwood on the evening train Saturday. We had six little ducks hatch this morning. Had string beans for dinner yesterday.

Friday, July 12   Pleasant. I did my work and my ironing and got some things ready so I could go to Norwood. I was so tired toward night I could hardly move. Went up stairs and laid down on the bed in the big room for a while. Went to bed early.

Saturday, July 13   Pleasant. I did up my work and got ready to come to Norwood. (Guy and the horses.) Irma came down town with me. We left the baby at Mr. Carter's and I stopped at the cemetary with some flowers. Got letters from Edith and Mr. R. Came down to Norwood on the 6:33 train. (Checking my satchel.) Edie and I went over street after supper. Had bananas, chocolates, and peanuts. Saw most of the young men I am acquainted with.

Sunday, July 14   Pleasant. I went to church with Aunt Mercy and Edie. After dinner, I wrote my letters. Then we went for a walk over to Hat's. Edie, Eva, Hazel and I went for a long walk. We went to church again in the evening. It was real warm. Staid to Sunday school in the morning.

Monday, July 15   Pleasant and warm. I helped do up the work, went over street with my letters and pictures, read some in the forenoon. In the afternoon Edie and I drove to Norfolk, staid to Mr. Farnsworth's to supper and looked the village over. Had a very pleasant ride. We all went over to Mr. Mott's in the evening.

Tuesday, July 16   Pleasant and warm. I helped do up the work and read quite a little while. Mrs. Mott came over in the afternoon. Ed went up to Net's. I heard Lee Wallace was dead. After supper Edie and I went up to Hat's, staid quite a little while then went over to Mr. Mott's, then down street and got some soda water. Walked home with Gertie. Stopped at the bakery a while and came home. I got a letter from Edith and Mr. R. We sat out under the trees in the afternoon.

Wednesday, July 17   Pleasant and warm. Helped do up the work and read some. About 10:30 we took a lunch and went up to Hat's. They took another lunch and Aunt Mercy, Edie, Hat, Eva, Hazel, and Pauline and I all went down on the bank of the river in the shade. We staid a while, then came back to the house. Arthur Farmer came up to see Edie.

Thursday, July 18   Pleasant and very warm. I laid down for a little while and read quite a bit. Edie and I were going for a boat ride but didn't go. We went over street after some berries. Mrs. Mott and Gertie were there to supper. Mr. Mott and Mr. Dawson came over after supper. I went up to Hat's to stay all night. Edie walked up with me.

Friday, July 19   Pleasant and quite a bit cooler. I staid at Hat's all day. Read some. After supper Hat and I drove out to the paper mill. Had a pleasant ride. Saw some gypsies. We called at Leona's, got some flowers there. After we got back I took the horse down to the barn. Then we walked over to Mr. Mott's and bade Levitt and Gertie good bye for they are to start for Boston the next morning. I got a letter from Edith.

Saturday, July 20   Pleasant. I staid to Hat's until after dinner, then came back to Ed's. Read some. Laid down in the forenoon I was so sleepy. Grace Lunderman and Maud Welch came to see Edie, both staid to supper. Hat and the children came down after supper and we all went down street. I saw Mr. Bonham. We went down to the train to see the governor. We got some soda water in the evening.

Sunday, July 21   Pleasant. Edie and I went to church in the morning. After dinner I read a while, then we started for the cemetary, stopped at Hat's and ate ice cream. Aunt Mercy and I drove out to the cemetary and took some flowers. We found Ed there and he came back with us. I called on Mrs. Adams a few minutes. Aunt Mercy and I went to church, then called at Mr. Cassada's to see Nell. Then went home and ate a lunch and went to bed.

Monday, July 22   Pleasant and warm. I came home on the 7 o'clock train in the morning. Did my business in Canton and rode home with Mr. Pitt. I found a paper and letter from Mr. R. here for me and a letter from Larnard. I ate dinner in Mert's part, put my things away and wrote some letters. Lee Wallace is not dead.

Tuesday, July 23   Pleasant. I did part of my work and then walked down to the corner to mail two letters. Went up to Mrs. Bluett's a few minutes and took her paper home. Came back and finished my work. Laid down a while in the afternoon. Mert and Irma went to the village in the afternoon. I picked a lot of flowers from the garden and made five bouquets. They were lovely.

Wednesday, July 24   Quite pleasant but smoky. Late in the afternoon it grew real cool. I baked a loaf of bread and some oatmeal cookies. Had a good cooked dinner. After dinner I went down to the cemetary and took four bouquets. They were so pretty. I walked along with Irma and the baby. They went down to Mrs. Carter's. I got a letter from Edith. Two gentlemen called who were enlarging pictures and I let them take Papa's and Mama's to enlarge for Mert. Had to send up to Aunt Louise's to get the pictures. Both of the gentlemen were very pleasant.

Thursday, July 25   Pleasant. I picked a bouquet for myself. Walked down to the corner with the mail. I had a letter and Irma had a letter and two photographs. I was early so sat down on the side of the road to wait. Mert went to the village. Aunt Louise came over and spent the afternoon with me. I was surprised. Had the baby in here twice for quite a while.

Friday, July 26   Pleasant. Mert went to Plum Brook with a load of cheese boxes for Mr. Wallace. I swept and dusted the chambers and swept the sitting room. I was tired. Laid down toward night. Read some in the evening.

Saturday, July 27   Pleasant. Just at night it began to rain a little. I dusted and mopped up the oilcloths,[59] dusted the parlor, sitting room, and bedroom. Walked down to the corner after the mail in the afternoon. Got a letter from Edith. Got a letter from Mert Beswick asking about renting the farm. Didn't get any letter from St. Louis and I am so afraid something has happened. In fact I am sure something has happened and I am so worried. Took a bath in the afternoon and slicked up. Zuar went through the yard with Boyden's team over to fix fence.

Sunday, July 28   Rained most all day and last night too I guess. The sun shone out a little. I read after I got the work done up. I felt sick and had to lie down most all the afternoon. Wrote my letters in the evening. I got real interested in the book I am reading, "Her Dearest Foe."[60]

Monday, July 29   Pleasant in the forenoon, but rained in the afternoon hard. Mert, Irma, the baby, and Guy all went away in the afternoon. I did my work and in the afternoon finished the book I was reading. Mr. Tucker called to see if the farm is to be rented. Oh, I am so lonesome. How I wish I could hear from St. Louis.

Tuesday, July 30   Cloudy and rainy in the forenoon, but cleared off in the afternoon. I did my work then fussed around. Hardly know what to do nowadays. I am in such an unsettled state of mind. It is so hard. I laid down after dinner. It was very warm and sultry. The baby cried hard in the afternoon so finally I went and got her and brought her in here. She was as good as could be, was in here two hours and more. I sat out on the porch after supper. It was lovely. Irma sat there too.

Wednesday, July 31   Pleasant until toward night when it began to rain. Very windy. I did up my work and picked eight bouquets from my flower garden and arranged them. In the afternoon I went down to the cemetary and took my bouquets, seven of them. Rode with Mr. Packard. Stopped and got the mail when I came back. Got a letter from Edith and one from Larnard and Mr. Robert's picture and two St. Louis papers. I was glad to get some news from Mr. R. again.

AUGUST

Thursday, Aug. 1   Very pleasant in the morning and cool but clouded up after a while, was real cool all day. I walked down to the corner with my letters in the morning. Mert went to Potsdam, Irma and the baby went away. They were all gone about all day. Guy went hunting in the afternoon. I laid down a while. After supper I went for a walk, went up in the pasture and staid a long time. It was grand out, so still, not a leaf stirring. The sunset was fine too.

Friday, Aug. 2   Very pleasant. I did up my work and looked out some of the things that Mert is to have and got them together. I gave him some books. After dinner I took a bath and slicked up, had to wait until Jim Lindley came along to get some crackers and lemons then went up to

Mr. Boyden's. Grandma Boyden is sick in bed. Staid until after supper. Then Josie and Ruth brought me home.

Saturday, Aug. 3　　　　Rained a little bit in the morning but was very pleasant the rest of the day. Mert and Irma went to the village. I baked and did up my work. Walked down to the corner for the mail in the afternoon. Got a letter from Edith. Read some toward night and went to bed early.

Sunday, Aug. 4　　　　Very pleasant. I did up my work and read and wrote the rest of the day and evening. The rest went away as usual but Mert was here the most of the time. I wrote a long letter to Edith and three others.

Monday, Aug. 5　　　　Very pleasant. Just a perfect day. I did my work, read some etc. Had the baby in here a while in the afternoon. Laid down about an hour in the afternoon. After supper I walked up to see how Grandma Boyden was and called at Mr. Pitt's too.

Tuesday, Aug. 6　　　　Pleasant. I did up my work and got ready to go down town, went around the other way and took Cora's jacket home that I wore home last night. Called up to Mr. Gardner's and had a visit with Kittie and Marnie Crandall. Lena was not at home. When I came home, I drove up to Mr. Barrett's and paid him the ten dollars. Got a letter from Edith and a paper from Mr. Roberts.

Wednesday, Aug. 7　　　　Rained most all day. Cleared off just at night. I did my work, finished my book and made some biscuit in the forenoon. Went down for the mail in the afternoon. Got two letters from Mr. Roberts and bad news. I was so discouraged for a while but perhaps it will all turn out right at last.

Thursday, Aug. 8　　　　Pleasant until between 3 & 4, then a big storm came up, lasted quite a while. I walked down to the corner to mail my letters in the morning and to look for mail in the afternoon. Did my work and some mending and took a bath in the afternoon. Read toward night.

Friday, Aug. 9　　　　Pleasant. Just at night it began to sprinkle. I did up my work and read some and picked and arranged some bouquets for the cemetary in the forenoon. In the afternoon I walked down to the cemetary. Called on Jessie and then called at the Misses Rodee's and staid until Cora Pitt came along, then rode home with her. Read some in the evening.

Saturday, Aug. 10   Rainy. I worked most all day. Laid down in the afternoon. Then changed my dress and sat out on the porch after supper. Read in the evening.

Sunday, Aug. 11   Rained some in the morning but was pleasant the rest of the day. I did up my work, took a bath, and changed my clothes and walked up to Mr. Pitt's. Staid quite a while, then came home and finished reading "Mildred"[61] and wrote to Edith. Pearl Bluett came up to borrow two yeast cakes.

Monday, Aug. 12   Very pleasant. I hurried around in the morning and got ready to ride to town with Mr. Pitt. Paid for the headstones and lettering on monument. Went to county clerk's office and found out about the number of acres in the farm. We got home at 12:30. I ate dinner, fed the chickens and sewed a few carpet rags. Then walked down to see if there was any mail. Called at Mrs. Bluett's and then went up to Ira Bullis to call but staid to supper and until almost dark. Carrie was so kind to me.

Tuesday, Aug. 13   Very pleasant and quite warm. I did my washing, a big one. Was busy until about 4 o'clock doing what I have to do each day and my washing. Mrs. Bullis came over a little before 4 o'clock and staid until most dark. I walked down to the corner with her to get the mail. Got a letter from Edith. Had my tubs to empty and dishes to wash after I got back. Didn't get to bed until 10 o'clock.

Wednesday, Aug. 14   Pleasant and warm again. I did up my work. Then sprouted nearly two bushels of potatoes. After dinner I took a bath and nap and changed my clothes. Walked down to see if there was any mail but didn't find any. He must have forgotten it I think. Read a little, after supper got in my clothes and picked a lovely bouquet of sweet peas.

Thursday, Aug. 15   Pleasant most of the time but rained after dinner quite hard for a few minutes and sprinkled some afterward. About 11 o'clock, Uncle Ing and Uncle Austin came.[62] I got dinner for them and after dinner they drove up to Uncle Nelson's for a while. Then Uncle Ing went home and Uncle Austin staid here. He ate supper with me too. Just before dark I walked down to the mail box and got a letter and paper from Mr. Roberts. That letter made me feel better. I walked down this morning to send a letter to Edith.

Friday, Aug. 16   Pleasant. I did up my work and did my ironing and made a cake. Uncle Austin ate breakfast with me, went down to

Carter's and staid to dinner, came back about 2 o'clock and ate supper with Mert and Irma. I also baked bread today. Had the baby for quite a while after supper. Got a letter from Edith and it was such a sad one. We had green corn for dinner.

Saturday, Aug. 17   Pleasant. I did my Saturday's work and in the afternoon took a bath and walked down to the corner to see if there was any mail. Uncle Austin went up to Mr. Boyden's and staid to dinner but was here to breakfast and supper with me. Mert and Irma went to Potsdam and to Uncle Ing's. Mert brought home his stuffed blue heron. It looks very nice. I picked a beautiful bouquet of sweet peas.

Sunday, Aug. 18   Pleasant. Just a lovely day. I did up my work and picked and arranged some flowers, had a lovely bouquet of zinnias. Read in the afternoon some. Wiped the dishes for Irma after dinner. Uncle Austin went up to Uncle Nelson's and staid for dinner but was here to breakfast and supper. The rest were all gone in the evening so if Uncle Austin hadn't been here I would have been all alone.

Monday, Aug. 19   Pleasant. Uncle Austin was here all day except to take my mail down to the corner for me and take a walk. I got a good dinner and made a lovely tapioca pudding and cooked some beans for supper. Walked down to the corner for the mail in the afternoon. Arthur Wallace came over here. He staid to dinner with Mert and called on me.

Tuesday, Aug. 20   Quite pleasant, a little cloudy and rained a little. Uncle Austin went up to Uncle Nelson's and staid all day. I did up my work in good shape. Then undressed and went to bed for about two hours. Then took a bath and changed my clothes. I walked down to the corner to look for the mail but didn't find any. Uncle Austin and I sat out on the porch and talked for a long time just at night. Mert and Irma went to the village in the afternoon.

Wednesday, Aug. 21   Pleasant and very warm. About 11 o'clock Uncle Austin and I started for town. We staid until between 4 & 5. Came home around by Langdon's. Went down by the Barnes factory as they are fixing the straight road. We stopped at the cemetary. Uncle Austin treated me to soda water. I called at Lena's on Mrs. Kilbourn and Mrs. Gillett. Mrs. G. served me lunch, cake, cheese, peaches and iced tea. Heard that Jim McMinn is coming the last of the week. Marvie, Fannie, and Aunt Laurinda came here while we were gone, then went over to Aunt Laurinda's.

Thursday, Aug. 22   Pleasant and hot in the morning but began to thunder and lightening before noon and rained very hard nearly all the P.M. and thundered very hard. Walter Boyden called on me, he was down with the men on the road. I got letters from Edith and Mr. R., good ones as they always are. Got Mr. Wells bill. Uncle Austin went to Aunt Laurinda's.

Friday, Aug. 23   Rained very hard most of the afternoon. I was sick in the morning, could hardly do my work but did. Uncle Austin went down to Mr. Carter's, came back in the afternoon. Aunt Laurinda, Marvie and Fannie came over. Mert and Marvie went to the village and didn't get back until late. Aunt Laurinda staid all night. They ate dinner and supper with me. I had lots of good things to eat.

Saturday, Aug. 24   Pleasant. Aunt L. went home. Uncle A. went up to Uncle Nelson's. I did a big day's work and had the house as slick as it could be. Mert and Irma took some of their things down to Carter's. I gave Mert quite a few things that belonged to him. Got a letter from Edith, a good one. Didn't go to the mail box yesterday, so Mert got the mail this morning. I was tired at night. Uncle A. and I played dominoes in the evening.

Sunday, Aug. 25   A beautiful day and a beautiful moonlight evening. I read some and talked with Uncle Austin. Grace and Walter Boyden and little Minnie Alford came down toward night and staid a little while. Uncle A. asked me to go to Ogdensburg tomorrow with him. Marvie and Fannie called here on their way home.

Monday, Aug. 26   Just a perfect day. I did my work up in good shape. Got ready to go to Ogdensburg and Uncle Austin and I started just in time to drive down there. Had a fine drive, just in good time. We arrived safe and sound, had a pleasant trip. In the afternoon Eva and I went up street to a dressmaker's then called at William Earl's. In the evening we called at Mrs. Martin's. I had a very pleasant day.

Tuesday, Aug. 27   Pleasant and warm. In the forenoon, we called at Lula's. In the afternoon we walked down to the hospital,[63] a lovely walk, Uncle Austin, Eva, Miss Martin and I. We girls walked back too. Saw George and John. We went through the buildings and were entertained by one of the insane men playing and singing. In the evening we went up to Uncle William's and spent the evening. George Johnston came up and came home with me. We went over to an ice cream social and each got a dish of ice cream. Had a very pleasant day.

Wednesday, Aug. 28   Very pleasant. In the forenoon, we rode up street with George. I drove the team. We went to the dressmaker's and to three or four stores. In the afternoon we went over to Prescott, Uncle Austin and Estace, Lula and Lily and I. Had a fine time. Went to Mr. Throope's. Met the Misses Lulu and Lily and Mr. Fred and Mr. and Mrs. T. Throope. Came back just at dusk. It was fine on the water. Went into a drugstore while we were waiting for a car and got some soda water. In the evening George and John came up. Mr. J. and I spent most of the evening out in the moonlight.

Thursday, Aug. 29   Pleasant. Took the 9:50 train for home. Uncle Austin and Eva went to the depot with me. George stopped in the morning and came over to the depot and gave me a sack of fruit. Saw Mr. and Mrs. Andrews at the depot. They were going home too. Had to wait at DeKalb 40 minutes or more. Mert and Irma came down town and I rode home with them. Got a letter from Mr. R. and found Edith's letter here waiting for me. I was awful tired. Had letters to write in the evening. Saw Jim McMinn go past the hotel.

Friday, Aug. 30   Pleasant. I did my work and my mending. Had quite a visit with Jim Lindley when he came along. Rode down to the corner with him and got the mail. Mert went to the village. I got a letter from Mr. R. It was a beautiful moonlight night when I went to bed. Helen Sawyer called on me. I went down to the corner to mail some letters in the morning and as it was raining called at Mrs. Poole's at the factory.

Saturday, Aug. 31   Rained all day more or less. Mert came in and talked with me about settling up and I am afraid he is going to make trouble for he wants a big price. It has made me feel very badly. Mert and I went to the village in the afternoon to see Mr. Hale but he wasn't there. I went up to Lena's and we went down street. I saw Jim McMinn. He is just the same as ever. He said he would come up and see me in the evening but it rained hard.

SEPTEMBER

Sunday, Sept. 1   Rained all day. I was so lonesome. Guy went over to see if he could get Aunt Laurinda to come over but he drove clear to North Russell and then didn't find her. I got dinner and waited a long time. Wrote to little Kathleen. I started a letter to Mr. R. but couldn't compose myself to finish it as I felt so restless. I drove down to see if Anna Wallace would come up and stay all night with me. She came. Yesterday I got the news that Edith's baby was born. Her name is Helene Mabel. I feel proud.

Monday, Sept. 2   It cleared off. Was cloudy part of the time, then the sun shone out and it was nice. Anna staid all day. I carried her home at night and drove over for Aunt Laurinda. She came home with me. Mert and Irma were moving all day.[64] Zuar drove in and talked with Mert.

Tuesday, Sept. 3   Pleasant. Mert and Irma were up here all day finishing up their moving. I worked most all day and was real tired. Aunt Laurinda staid. I am nearly discouraged. Some man called selling essences and medicine.[65]

Wednesday, Sept. 4   Pleasant and very warm. Aunt Laurinda and I went to town in the morning. I went and saw Mr. Hale. Saw Mr. Bullis and Mr. Wallace on business. Both of the Mr. Bullises were very kind to me. A Mr. Hayes was here to dinner. He is around testing milk. I got a paper and picture from St. Louis.

Thursday, Sept. 5   Pleasant and warm. I did a big washing and was tired. Aunt Mercy, Hat, and Pauline called here on their way back from Kate Mahoney's wedding. After supper I walked up to Mr. Pitt's. Didn't get back until after dark. Had my clothes lines all full of clothes. Our factory burned to the ground last night. Mr. Poole's folks lost everything and barely got out. We didn't know anything about it until this morning.

Friday, Sept. 6   Pleasant. I walked down to the corner with two letters and found the mail in the box. Got a letter from Edith and one from Mr. R. and Lena's postal. Called at Mrs. Bluett's. Did quite a lot of work, baking etc. After supper I drove down for Lena and carried Aunt Laurinda home. Talked with Mr. Hale. Lena and I didn't get home until after dark.

Saturday, Sept. 7　　　　Pleasant. I did up my Saturday's work and in the afternoon went down town. Took Lena with me and brought her back. Mert went down too. We went to see Mr. Hale. Such a time. Mert won't settle for less than 45 dollars an acre. I was so disappointed and angry. Was so angry could hardly hold myself. Life is so hard and I am so discouraged.

Sunday, Sept. 8　　　　Pleasant and cool. Just a delightful day. I did up the work with Lena's help. After dinner Lena and I started to walk up to church to the Mills, but stopped at Mr. Pitt's and Cora hitched up and we all went. Came around the other way home. Had a lovely drive. We stayed at Mr. Pitt's a while.

Monday, Sept. 9　　　　Pleasant and cool. I did up my work or Lena and I did. Sent my letters by Mr. Pitt. Guy and Mert went to the village in the forenoon. Mr. Hale sent for me to come down in the afternoon so Lena and I went. Mr. Hale has fixed it now so they can't sell the farm away from me. We didn't get home until after dark. Then we ate quite a supper and went to bed.

Tuesday, Sept. 10　　　　Pleasant and warmer. I did quite a lot of work. I got so tired and nervous thinking about the business I felt almost sick. Lena and I walked down to get the mail but just got a paper. I went up to Mr. Pitt's in the morning a few minutes. Mert came up in the afternoon and I talked with him and kissed him and felt better. Toward night, Lena and I drove down town to get Mr. Jackson to come up and see a cow that has a sore foot.

Wednesday, Sept. 11　　　　Rained all day. I walked down to mail a letter in the morning and down for the mail in the afternoon. Got a fine letter from Edith. Mert came up in the morning. Mr. Jackson came up to see the cow that got hurt. I worked all day and was tired. Lena and I played dominoes in the evening.

Thursday, Sept. 12　　　　Rained most all day. Lena and I walked down to the corner to mail a letter but were too late for the stage so I sent it by the free delivery rig. Mert came up and was here to dinner. He had to go back when it was raining hard. Lena and I read in the evening. We were all alone. I got a chance to read a little in the afternoon too.

Friday, Sept. 13　　　　It cleared off and the sun shone today. Guy went over to the Potsdam fair and Mert came up to milk. He staid to supper. I began to feel sick in the afternoon and felt real bad and had to go to bed early. Did quite a big day's work and baking. Lena went down after the mail for me. Got a good letter from Edith and my St. Louis paper. (Edith's birthday.)

Saturday, Sept. 14   Pleasant. Mert came up here and he and Lena and I went to the village. Lena went home. Mert and I stayed all day to fix up our business, and we have agreed to settle at Mert's price. That is a relief to me. I carried Mert up to Mr. Mead's when we came home as he had agreed to do the milking there. I drove over after Aunt Laurinda when I got back. Got a fine letter from Mr. Roberts. I was so tired when I got home I felt just like crying.

Sunday, Sept. 15   Rained quite a bit but was pleasant part of the time. Aunt Laurinda staid all day and all night. Mert came up and brought me the bills, the blacksmith's and grain bills. Aunt L. and I were here to dinner alone. Grace and Walter Boyden were here a little while. I felt sick and lonesome all day. Was in pain all day. Heard that Ella Winslow's little baby is dead. I wrote a long letter to Edith.

Monday, Sept. 16   Rained a little but was pleasant most of the time only the wind blew a hurricane. I carried Aunt L. home in the forenoon. Mert was up in the morning. Dwight Boyden came over and helped Guy milk and was here to supper. They went away after supper. I walked down to see if there was any mail and went up to H. Bullis a few minutes and Birdie Crary came over to stay all night with me. I laid down a little while in the afternoon.

Tuesday, Sept. 17   Rained hard until about three o'clock in the afternoon, then it cleared off and the sun shone. Birdie Crary went home in the morning. I did my work and made a cake and pie. Got a letter from Edith. Mr. McClellan's house burned this morning about four o'clock. I laid down a while in the afternoon. This is the first night I have been alone with just Guy.[66] I wrote a long letter to Mr. Roberts and one to Ella.

Wednesday, Sept. 18   Pleasant and cool. I did up my work and swept the chambers. Mert was up a little while in the morning. He took my letters to mail. Carrie Bullis and Birdie Crary and the children drove in, and just at night Inez Gibson, Bessie Moore and Hazel Runions drove in. I walked down to the corner for the mail in the afternoon. Was all alone in the evening and so lonesome. Got a letter from Aunt Mercy.

Thursday, Sept. 19   Pleasant. Guy went to the fair[67] and I was alone all day. I did quite a bit of work. Had roasted corn for dinner, the first I have had this year. I changed my clothes in the afternoon and walked down for the mail. Guy came home to milking and I took the rig and drove up to Mr. Aldrich's and McClellan's. Guy went back down to the show and I went down and staid with Lena. We nearly froze coming home. It was very cold. Came four in the buggy.

Friday, Sept. 20   Pleasant. I worked about all day, was tired when night came. Mert came up in the afternoon and brought up the mail. I got letters from Edith and Mr. Roberts. Just got the work done up and was thinking of going to bed when Bert Earl, Lula and the baby came. I got supper for them and visited for quite a while. I was glad to have them come.

Saturday, Sept. 21   Very pleasant. I did quite a bit of work. Mert came up in the forenoon to go to the village. Bert, Lula and the baby went up to Uncle Nelson's to dinner and for the afternoon. I hurried around with my work, took a bath and got ready to go down town. Mert and I went, Mr. Hale wasn't there so we couldn't do that business. I did my trading and we hurried home. I took care of my horse and got supper before Guy came in and did some work besides. Washed some windows. Bert and his folks came back.

Sunday, Sept. 22   Very pleasant. I worked all the forenoon up until about 2 o'clock. Had to do some things I couldn't get done yesterday. I had a good dinner. Soon after dinner Bert's folks started for home. Mr. Bluett called in the afternoon and Ralph Willard called to see about renting the farm. I picked a lovely bouquet of sweet peas. This is Mama's birthday. Got a letter from Eva yesterday.

Monday, Sept. 23   Very pleasant but windy. I worked all day. Laid down a little while before supper. I walked down for the mail by moon light. Got a letter from Mr. Hale. Sent my mail by Mr. Pitt and talked a while with him this morning. I was all alone in the evening, wrote to Mr. R. and read a while.

Tuesday, Sept. 24   Pleasant. Dwight came to help Guy get in the corn. I did my work, made a pie and some applesauce. Walked down to the corner to mail Mr. R.'s letter, called at Mrs. Bluett's while waiting for the stage. Laid down in the afternoon and had a good rest. Walked down for the mail by moonlight again. Got letters from Edith and Aunt Mercy.

Read a while in the evening. It was real cold with indications of frost, so I brought in the ripe cucumbers.

Wednesday, Sept. 25   Pleasant and quite cool. I did a big washing and quite a lot of other work besides. Baked bread and cake. I was very tired. Mert came up a while in the morning. I talked with him quite a bit, was alone in the evening. Read quite a bit.

Thursday, Sept. 26   Pleasant. Worked all day. Sold the pig to Mr. Clark. I was very tired. Walked down for the mail by moonlight. Got a letter from Edith and my "Ladies' Home Journal." Read a while in the evening. Was all alone. Mert came up in the forenoon. Mr. Wells grist mill burned last night.

Friday, Sept. 27   Very pleasant. I did up my work and got ready to go to the village. Mert and I went. I got my new hat and it just suits me, and I got the cloth for my jacket and skirt and sent it up to Mrs. Griffith's to be made. Got a fine letter from Mr. Roberts. It just did me good.

Saturday, Sept. 28   Pleasant. Guy had to go to town early with the pig, so I had to go to the factory. Stopped and got Grace Boyden to ride over with me. Saw Tom Carter up to Mr. Pitt's. Got dinner and did up the work, then went to Canton again, Mert and I. I got letters from Edith and Mr. Roberts. Felt sad and discouraged tonight.

Sunday, Sept. 29   Pleasant until along in the afternoon then it grew cloudy and just at chore time it just poured. Guy and his girl went up to his folks and got back here just as it began to rain hard. She staid here until after chores and supper and they staid a while in the evening because it rained so. I wrote long letters to Edith and Mr. R. and it was lots of company for me.

Monday, Sept. 30   Pleasant and cooler. I did up my work and in the afternoon drove down town. I went alone. Mert took Irma with Carter's rig. We staid just a few minutes as they weren't ready to finish up the business. I am getting so tired of going down town so much. Sent my letter by Miltie Pitt this morning.

OCTOBER

Tuesday, Oct. 1   Pleasant. Guy was gone all day mostly. I had dinner all alone. Did my work and read a little. Laid down a while in the afternoon. Walked down for the mail. Got a letter from Edith and one of dear little Kathleen's curls. Went to bed early. Clint Barsett was down to see about renting the farm.

Wednesday, Oct. 2   Rained most all day. Cleared off toward night and was lovely out. I did my work, laid down a little while in the afternoon. This is my birthday, and I wasn't forgotten even if my dear mother wasn't here to give me something. I got a book from Edith, "The Prince of the House of David."[68] It brought the tears to my eyes for I have heard Mama speak so often about reading that when she was a girl. I got a lovely diary for 1902, a souvenir of St. Louis and a map of St. Louis showing site of world's fair etc. from Mr. R. He didn't forget me either.

Thursday, Oct. 3   Pleasant most of the time, had a few little showers. I walked down to the corner to mail my letters but was too late for the stage. Walked up to Mrs. Bluett's and waited a few minutes to see if I could get a chance to send them but had to bring them back home as I got left all around. I worked all the rest of the day, made some doughnuts. Made what few ripe cucumbers I had into pickles. Walked down for the mail in the afternoon.

Friday, Oct. 4   Pleasant and real cool. I walked down with my letters again and sent them this morning. Called at Mrs. Bluett's while waiting for the stage. Worked most all day, baked bread. Mr. Jackson called here, was going up to Mr. Pitt's. Jim Lindley came along with groceries and took my two little kittens home with him. I am all alone tonight and miss them for they were lots of company. Walked down for the mail in the afternoon.

Saturday, Oct. 5   Quite pleasant but cold until just at night, when it began to rain. I did my work up, took my time. Mame Bullis stopped here in the afternoon selling Christmas books. Guy went to look up threshers. It was kind of a queer day, seems as though I was busy all the time and then didn't get much done. Got a letter from Mr. R. Edith's letter didn't come yesterday or today. I am so sorry. It must be delayed in some way. Mert was up in the morning.

Sunday, Oct. 6   Rain in the morning but cleared off nicely. Was real cold. I was alone all day. Read the book through that Edith sent me, "intra mures."[69] Mame Mott called to get the book Edith sent Aunt Mercy and Mama's veil and bonnet that Aunt Mercy wanted to take. I had a crying spell after I let her take it. Oh, I am so lonely and sad. Dwight was here to supper with Guy.

Monday, Oct. 7   Pleasant. I did my work and washed the windows in the other part inside and out. Kept busy all day. Finished Edith's letter. Mert was up twice in the morning and afternoon. Got Edith's letter. Was alone in the evening.

Tuesday, Oct. 8   Pleasant and warmer. I did my work, took up some plants in my flower garden. Read some. Walked down for the mail and rode back with Mabel Hunt and another girl. Got a letter from Mrs. Griffith saying for me to come and try on my jacket. Guy went to the village to get some grain for the horses, groceries and oil etc. I sent letters to Edith, Mr. R. and Bert. Mr. Gibson stopped here. Flora Taylor Barsett drove down to see what conclusion I had come to about renting the farm.

Wednesday, Oct. 9   Pleasant. I did the common work and made some cookies and baked some beans and cooked some little potatoes for the hens. Mert came up in the afternoon and brought the mail. I got a letter from Edith. I laid down a while in the afternoon then took a bath. Wrote to Edith in the evening.

Thursday, Oct. 10   Pleasant. I did up my work and went to town. Mert rode from the corner down to Carter's with me and cut a whip for me, as our whip was lost and I couldn't make Fred horse go good. I went up to Mrs. Griffith's to try on my jacket and had quite a visit with her. Went up to see Mr. Hale. Everyone was good to me today. Got letters from Mr. R. and Mabel Lewis and a postal from that picture company. We had quite a shower soon after I got home. Dolly Boyden came along here and stopped and Guy carried her home.

Friday, Oct. 11   Pleasant and warm. I did up my work then got ready to go to town. Mert went with me. The paper hadn't come back from Edith so we couldn't finish up business today either. I was tired and my head ached. Got a letter from Bert Earl. It is so hard all around for me. I was alone in the evening and lonesome.

Saturday, Oct. 12   Pleasant and real warm. I worked hard all day every minute. Swept and dusted most all day. I worked all day, then there was lots I didn't get done that I wanted to do. Went down for the mail just at dark. Got letters from Edith and Mr. R. and a bill from Dr. Madill. Just after dark Bert's folks came. I was very tired. It seemed as if I couldn't keep going. We sat up and talked until 11 o'clock then I had a little work to do up stairs before I could go to bed.

Sunday, Oct. 13   Rained most all day. Bert's folks couldn't go home on account of the weather. I was sick all day, felt bad. Had to lie down a while and couldn't half do my work. Made biscuits for dinner, and they were fine.

Monday, Oct. 14   Very pleasant. Bert's folks started for home about a quarter to 11. I worked all day. Picked up things in the other part. Ella Boyden came down in the afternoon and staid a little while. She brought me some snow apples and took back some crab apples. Some man drove in here to rent the farm. I walked down to the corner in the afternoon to look for the mail but didn't find any. Mert came up in the morning.

Tuesday, Oct. 15   Very pleasant but cold. Guy went over to get the horse shod in the forenoon. I did my work and Mert and I went down town in the afternoon but Mr. Hale hadn't come back from New York so we couldn't do any business. I went up to Mrs. Griffith's and tried on my jacket. It is going to be pretty. I drove over for Aunt Laurinda when I came from the village as I want her to help me tomorrow. Have got so much to do I don't know what to do first.

Wednesday, Oct. 16   It rained all day quite hard. Aunt Laurinda did my big washing. Mert came up in the forenoon for me to go down in the afternoon. He went down in the morning to see if Mr. Hale had come first. So I went and left my work and we finally have got settled. I paid all the debts I could down there. We didn't get home until 9 o'clock. I was bound I would do all I could before I started for home. Got letters from Edith and Bert.

Thursday, Oct. 17   Rained most all day. Aunt Laurinda and I did a big day's work. Worked all day long. Mr. Pitt brought up my mail from the mailbox. I got two papers and pictures from Mr. R. and the receipt from Dr. Russell. Guy went to the village in the afternoon and when he came back Dwight was with him and did the chores and Guy staid in the horse barn. I am glad I haven't got to stay alone here much longer.

Friday, Oct. 18   Cold and cloudy. Rained and snowed some. Mert came up to bid me good bye in the morning as he is going to Buffalo tonight. How I hated to have him go. I cried hard and brought on a sick nervous headache. Guy went away in the evening and I was left alone. I read until I got sleepy then went to bed. Hadn't been there long when I heard double wagons stop and knew it was Bert moving out.[70] Had to get up and start a fire, get supper and fix a bed for them. There was Bert, John Nichols, Roy Johnston and Jud Kennedy.

Saturday, Oct. 19   Cloudy and rainy. I drove down town, expected to meet Lula and the baby but they didn't come. I got my new jacket at Mrs. Griffith's. It is very pretty. Had another visit with her. Got letters from Edith, Mr. Roberts, Dr. Madill and Mr. Hale. (Edith's letter enclosed.) Got real wet going down. Saw Lena on the street.

Sunday, Oct. 20   Pleasant and cool. Guy left today, and Bert began work. I had quite a bit of work to do today as I was gone yesterday. Took a bath in the afternoon. Will and Marvie called. I wrote to Edith in the evening.

Monday, Oct. 21   Cloudy and cold in the forenoon but cleared off in the afternoon. I went down town after Lula and the baby. Guy rode with me. I paid him, got some groceries, sent the $100 to Dr. Madill. Engaged a man to come up and fix the roof etc. then we came home. We all ate dinner in here and I also got supper for all of them. Tom Carter was down town and got my horse for me.

Tuesday, Oct. 22   Pleasant. Guy and Dolly stopped here in the morning. They were all in here to breakfast. Then they went to work for themselves so I was alone again. I slicked up the house a little. Walked down to the corner to see if there was any mail and called up to Mrs. Bluett's a little while. When I got back I found the men here with the pictures waiting for me. Paid for the pictures. That man gave me a souvenir of the Pan American.[71] Found out the threshers are all ready to come here, so I fixed the table for them, made a pan of doughnuts and dressed a pan of potatoes.[72]

Wednesday, Oct. 23   Pleasant in the forenoon and until about 3 o'clock then it rained quite hard for a while but came off pleasant again later. The threshers were here to breakfast and dinner. That cost me $4.50. Walked down to the corner for the mail. Got a letter from Edith and a lock of baby Helene's hair. Little Curly came home. Lula helped with the threshers. I am glad that job is over. I was so in hopes I would get a letter from Mert today but didn't.

Thursday, Oct. 24   Pleasant and cold. Sent Edith's letter and papers by the free delivery this morning. Did quite a bit of work. Curly and I walked down for the mail in the afternoon. Got a letter from Mr. R., a good one. Wrote him a long letter in the evening.

Friday, Oct. 25   Pleasant and cold. Walked down to the corner to mail Mr. R.'s letters and as it was so cold went in to Mrs. Bluett's to wait for the stage. Did up my work and took a bath. In the afternoon Lula and I drove down town to do some trading and came right back. Just as I was ready to start the two Mrs. Bullis and two children came to see me. They didn't stay as I was ready to go away. Got my "Ladies' Home Journal," two papers from St. Louis and my "Universalist Leader." Lula asked me out there to supper. We played dominoes in the evening.

Saturday, Oct. 26   Pleasant and quite a bit warmer. I did a big day's work. Washed the windows outside and in, swept, dusted, and mopped the oilcloths, steps and stone. Kept busy all day. Bert's folks started for Ogdensburg between 3 & 4 o'clock. Guy came down to milk. Just at night I walked down for the mail. Got a letter from Edith. Then I walked up to Mr. Pitt's as it was getting late and was afraid Guy wasn't coming. Called at Mrs. McCellan's too. Found 25 cents today right by the stove. Staid alone all night.

Sunday, Oct. 27   Very pleasant. How I wished someone would take me for a ride or come to see me. I was so lonesome. Guy came down to do the milking and ate breakfast with me. I read some and wrote some. Went for a walk up in the pasture in the afternoon and sat on the big stone by the brook. Everything is lovely out but I am so lonesome. I want my father, mother, sister and brother. God only knows how I want them and need them.

Monday, Oct. 28   Pleasant. It froze quite hard last night. I ironed quite a bit and starched a lot of white clothes. My pan of starch got afire. Had kerosene in it. I brought in the rest of the cabbage and the carrots today. It made my back ache hard to dig the carrots. Irma came up to see Lula this afternoon but didn't come in to see me at all. I walked down for the mail just at night. Got a letter from Mert. I was so glad. He sent me a souvenir of the Pan American, a name plate.

Tuesday, Oct. 29   Warm and pleasant. I sent a letter to Mert by free delivery. Did up my work, made some ginger cakes and sprinkled my starched clothes. After dinner and after I got the work done up I walked down to the cemetary and took two little sprigs of chrysanthemum, as those were all the flowers I had left for Papa and Mama. Took the letter Mert sent to Irma along down there. Saw Zuar this afternoon and talked a while with him. Mert sent me a souvenir of the Pan American. It came today and the receipt from Dr. Madill.

Wednesday, Oct. 30   Warm and pleasant. I did up my work, washed the windows up stairs and ironed the white clothes. Ate dinner with Bert's folks and in the afternoon Lula and I went to town. Had a nice drive. I got letters from Edith and Mr. R., fine ones. Mr. R.'s letter made me feel pretty good. Got the St. Louis paper.

Thursday, Oct. 31   Warm and pleasant. I walked down to the corner with my letters and waited on the side of the road for the stage. I was kind of late getting up this morning as I sat up so late writing last night. Ate breakfast with Bert's folks. Mame and Carrie Bullis and the children came over in the afternoon and staid a while. I got in turnips after they went away until just dark. Then I went down for the mail. Read a while in the evening.

NOVEMBER

Friday, Nov. 1   Pleasant but colder. It rained a little last night or early this morning but came off quite pleasant today. I did all sorts of things today. Walked down for the mail toward night. Found a cent out by the stove today.

Saturday, Nov. 2   Pleasant. I did my Saturday's work in the forenoon, ironed the starched colored clothes after dinner. Took a bath and changed my clothes. Tried on my brown dress, it fits lovely and I think I'll put a black yoke in it and wear it soon. Walked down for the mail just at night. Got letters from Edith and Mr. R. Bert and Lula went down town in the evening and the baby stayed with me. I undressed her and put her to bed and she slept all night with me.

Sunday, Nov. 3   Pleasant. I got up and built my fire and started my breakfast, then dressed the baby and we ate breakfast before her mother came down stairs. About noon we went for a drive, went clear up by the white church, went one way and came back another. Took a lunch and stopped in the woods to eat it. Went in the double buggy, Bert, Lula, the baby and I, and Curly and Bounce. Rather a late date for a picnic dinner but we enjoyed it. I ate a big dinner.

Monday, Nov. 4   Pleasant in the forenoon, but clouded up and grew real cold toward night. I walked down to the corner to mail my two letters and two sets of papers. Did a big washing. Had to bring my clothes in toward night as it was so windy and looked so much like rain. Walked down to look for mail just at night but didn't find any. Mr. Wells came along and talked with me for quite a while.

Tuesday, Nov. 5   Pleasant. I made some oatmeal crackers and did my ironing, mopped up the oilcloths, pantry and big stove and did my common work. Had a boiled dinner today. In the afternoon Lula, the baby and I called at Mrs. Bluett's and the two young Mrs. Bullis'. Had a good walk. No mail today either.

Wednesday, Nov. 6   Pleasant and quite cool. I did up my work and commenced the Christmas stockings. Fixed the velveteen on the bottom of my checked skirt. Walked down for the mail in the afternoon. Got a letter from Edith and one from Carroll. Got a letter today for Papa. Oh, I feel so lonesome and sad tonight, so tired of everything. Life is so hard, so hard.

Thursday, Nov. 7   Pleasant. I got up and got my breakfast and ate it. Then I was so sick I could hardly hold my head up. Had to go and lie down. I waited to send Edith's letter by the free delivery rig. Then I laid down and stayed there until about 2 o'clock. Oh, how sick I was. It seemed as if I couldn't stand it. About 2 o'clock I got up and got my dinner and did up my work. Walked down for the mail then. Got a fine letter from Mr. R. and one from Lena and two St. Louis papers and a picture.

Friday, Nov. 8   Pleasant. I rode to the factory with Bert and took my two letters down to mail. Called at Mrs. Bluett's while waiting for the stage. I didn't do much in the forenoon. Ate dinner with Bert's folks and took out soup enough for everyone. In the afternoon I brought in lots of limbs from across the road and put them down cellar to have in the winter to start fires with. Walked down for the mail just at night. I was so glad, the deed sent up from Mr. Hale's office. Got a letter from Mert.

Saturday, Nov. 9   Pleasant. I baked bread, cookies and beans and muffins. Did up my Saturday's work and slicked up. In the afternoon Lula's brother and father came to see her. Her father was drunk when he got here. Dear me, how it made me feel to have anyone come here like that. I felt so discouraged. Lula and I drove up to the Mills just at night as she wanted to get some sugar. Then I drove down for the mail after that. I got another fine letter from Mr. R. One sentence in it made me happy.

Sunday, Nov. 10   Very cold but pleasant. They all went up to Uncle Nelson's to dinner and Curly and I stayed alone. I was out with them last evening and we played dominoes. Was out there a little while this evening. I wrote three letters in the evening to Mert, Edith and Mr. R. Went to bed in pretty good season.

Monday, Nov. 11   Pleasant and cold but grew warmer and snowed quite hard and turned to rain at night. Lula and I went down town and were out in the snow storm. Had a lot of "experiences." I ate supper with Bert's folks and in the evening Bert, Lula, Mr. Nichols and I went for a walk. Then Mr. N. and I took a little extra walk.[73] Got a letter from Aunt Mercy.

Tuesday, Nov. 12   Rained hard all day long. I ate dinner out with them and they all ate supper in here with me but Lula furnished part of the supper. We played dominoes in the afternoon and evening. I walked down to look for mail in the rain and mud and then didn't find any.

Wednesday, Nov. 13   The ground was all covered with snow this morning, and it has snowed all day and been cold. The boys went down and got the mail for me. I got two letters from Edith and one from Mr. Roberts. I ate breakfast and dinner with them and supper. I wrote two letters in the evening and then we played dominoes. Uncle Nelson came down in the forenoon and came in to see me and staid quite a while.

Thursday, Nov. 14   Snowed all day. I didn't do much work for I was visiting the most of the time with the rest of the folks. Laid down a while in the afternoon. Some fellow stopped here to get the cutter to go over to Little River and get his. I ate dinner and supper with them. We played dominoes in the evening.

Friday, Nov. 15   Pleasant mostly. Snowed some. The boys went to the woods and got a load of wood. I did quite a bit of patching. Ate dinner and supper with them. We had popcorn in the evening. Mr.

Nichols came in and spent the evening with me and told me something that surprised me. I must be an awful girl. I did the most of my Saturday's work today.

Saturday, Nov. 16   Pleasant. Bert took old Mr. Nichols home, and Lula's brother staid to do the chores until Bert came back. I patched quite a bit. Ate dinner out there. We played dominoes in the evening. Mr. N. went down and got the mail for me. I got letters from Mr. R., Edith, Larnard, and one from that man that plastered here.

Sunday, Nov. 17   Pleasant. I ate dinner with Lula and her brother and the baby. Didn't do anything all day only sit around and talk. Mr. Nichols was in here most all day and in the evening. I like him, he is so kind and nice to talk with. (Sunday evening.)

Monday, Nov. 18   Pleasant and mild. Snowed in the evening, though. I tried to write some letters but was so tired I couldn't collect my thoughts and everything. I ate supper with them. Mr. Nichols and I went for a sleigh ride after chores. Then he spent the evening with me. I patched some and laid down a little while in the afternoon. I undressed the baby tonight and held her quite a while as she wanted me to.

Tuesday, Nov. 19   Pleasant. I did up my work and got my mail ready to send and patched stockings. Ate dinner with Bert's folks. Mr. Nichols went home today. Lula carried him down to the 4 o'clock train. I did up her work, washed both the breakfast and dinner dishes. Then I laid down with little Lula and she went to sleep. Went to bed early for I was very tired.

Wednesday, Nov. 20   Very pleasant. I did my work up, got a cooked dinner, and made a cake and patched the rest of my stockings. Walked down for the mail in the afternoon. Got letters from Edith and Mr. Roberts. Lula got hurt this morning by a big icicle falling down on her head. The baby was in here a good share of the time today.

Thursday, Nov. 21   Very pleasant. I cleaned in the pantry. Worked all day and then had to leave part of it. I ate one meal with Bert's folks. Walked down for the mail just at night but didn't find any.

Friday, Nov. 22   Pleasant. I did a big day's work. Finished cleaning the pantry and swept all over good in the sitting room and two bedrooms. Moved everything out and took up all the rugs. Was tired at night. Walked down for the mail just at night. Got a letter from Mr.

Nichols. Went up stairs with Lula in the evening and sewed a little then went to bed.

Saturday, Nov. 23   Pleasant and cold. I worked all day and finished slicking up, looked very nice here when I got through. I walked down for the mail in the afternoon. Got letters from Edith and Lena. Mr. R.'s letter didn't come. I staid down stairs all night and kept a fire as it was quite cold.[74] Slept in the big rocking chair and in Mama's bed.

Sunday, Nov. 24   Rained a little in the forenoon and turned to sleet in the afternoon, then it rained hard and froze on. I wrote seven letters. Ate breakfast and dinner in here and another dinner out there about 5 o'clock and a lunch of crackers and apples. Was tired when I got ready to go to bed after 11 o'clock.

Monday, Nov. 25   It snowed hard all day. I did up my work and got ready to go to town about 12 o'clock. Lula and I went and didn't get home until after dark. I mailed nine letters, eight that I wrote and one that I sent on to Mert. I did lots of little odd jobs down town.

Tuesday, Nov. 26   Cold and stormy all day. I worked on the babies Christmas stockings. Cooked quite a dinner today. I got one of those stockings done, and they will be pretty. I went to bed in pretty good season and slept good.

Wednesday, Nov. 27   The sun shone out good and the trees and grass and everything looked lovely, as if they were covered with diamonds. I worked on those stockings again. Bert got the mail, and I got two fine letters from Mr. R. and one from Edith. I answered them in the evening. Bert and Lula went down town after things for Thanksgiving and Midget, Curly and I staid at home.

Thursday, Nov. 28   Pleasant and cold. I missed sending my letters by the free delivery rig. I did up my work and had everything neat and nice, then took a bath and changed my clothes and ate Thanksgiving dinner with Bert's folks. We didn't have dinner until four o'clock. I walked down for the mail and it was cold. My hands and feet were very cold, they ached. Got a letter from Aunt Mercy.

Friday, Nov. 29   Pleasant and much warmer. Snowed some. After breakfast I started out to send my letters but missed the stage and several other chances and had to bring them back home but sent them by Mr. Boyden. I called at Mrs. Bluett's, the two Mrs. Bullis and Mrs. Hosley's on errands. Walked down for the mail at night and it was snowing very hard but was warm. I got three papers, my St. Louis paper among them. I walked about 3½ miles today.

Saturday, Nov. 30   Pleasant. I did up my work and sewed some. In the afternoon Mrs. McClellan and Polly came down. I made one pair of little stockings for the babies. I walked down for the mail and got letters from Edith and Mr. Roberts. I had a sick headache and went to bed early and about 10 o'clock woke up so sick and vomited like everything. I stayed awake between 2 and 3 o'clock.

DECEMBER

Sunday, Dec. 1   Very pleasant and mild. I didn't feel very well all day. I did up my work slowly and slicked up. Laid down a while in the forenoon. Just got ready to write my letters about 3 o'clock in the afternoon when Marvie and Fannie came. Then I got a cooked supper. In the evening the boys went up to Aunt Laurinda's and she came back and staid all night. I didn't get any chance to write. We didn't get to bed until 12 o'clock.

Monday, Dec. 2   Pleasant. Our company was here all day. We all visited. All ate dinner and supper with Bert's folks. Dwight Boyden asked us all to come over there in the evening, so we all went on the bobsleds, Bert, Marvie, Fannie, Lula, Baby, Aunt Laurinda, Curly and I. We had a good time. I walked down for the mail just at night.

Tuesday, Dec. 3   Pleasant, snowed some. The company all staid today too. Aunt Laurinda and Fannie dressed five chickens for me. Lula cooked one of them for dinner, and we all ate out there. I was sick in the morning. We visited all day again. We were all sleepy. Lula went down for the mail.

Wednesday, Dec. 4   Pleasant, snowed some. In the morning I walked down to the corner to mail my letters and papers. Stopped in at Carrie Bullis to get warm. Marvie and Fannie started for home about noon. Bert went over to the shop to get the horses shod and Aunt Laurinda went with him and was going home but they were so late getting around she came back and staid all night. Bert got the mail. I got letters from Mr. R., Edith, Carroll and Kathleen.

Thursday, Dec. 5   Pleasant. Sent my letters by the free delivery rig this morning. Aunt Laurinda went home with Bert when he went to the woods. I sewed after she went on the things for the babies Christmas. Walked down for the mail just at night. Got a big roll of papers from Mr. R., three papers, two very pretty pictures and a sheet of music. I read in the evening.

Friday, Dec. 6   Pleasant. I did up my work and worked on the babies Christmas things the rest of the day. Got my jar of butter. Walked down for the mail just at night. Went to bed early and had a good night's sleep.

Saturday Dec. 7   I did housework all day. Swept and dusted up stairs and down and mopped up the oilcloths, watered the plants and cleaned the lamps etc. It was real pleasant today. I walked down for the mail just at night. My letters didn't come and it made me lonesome and homesick. I was so late sending mine that probably they didn't write. I slept in Mama's bed.

Sunday, Dec. 8   Dull and cloudy all day, but didn't storm, was much warmer. I slept late this morning. Had to dust up stairs this morning as I didn't get it done last night. Wrote my letters in the afternoon. Bert's folks went up to Aunt Laurinda's today. Curly and I staid alone. It began to snow toward night. It turned to rain later and rained hard.

Monday, Dec. 9   Very pleasant. The sun shone and it was real warm. I washed from about 12 until in the evening and then wasn't through. Had the door open all day and hung out clothes bare headed. It grew colder at night though and snowed hard. I went down for the mail just at night. Got letters from Edith and Larnard. I was very tired at night. Took some catnip tea and went to bed.

Tuesday, Dec. 10   The wind blew a hurricane all day and it was real cold. I finished my washing and had to put all the clothes up stairs on top of each other. I slicked all up and carried in water and filled everything up. Was very tired again at night. It is such hard work to do all those things. I went down for the mail and could hardly walk on account of the awful wind. Bert brought a package from the mailbox this morning. It was Larnard's picture and a book, "Beauties of the Rockies."[75]

Wednesday, Dec. 11   Pleasant. I did my work and wrote letters. Went down for the mail in the afternoon. Got two letters from Mr. R. and Edith, one from Eva and one from Mr. Nichols. Eva's letter was an invitation to spend Christmas with her. I would like to go but suppose I can't. Bert and I drove down to the cemetary just at night and covered the rose bushes for the winter. I am so glad they are fixed for I have been worrying about them.

Thursday, Dec. 12   Very pleasant and warm. I did up my work and got ready to go to town. Started about 11 o'clock and didn't get back until dark. Put in a great day shopping. I had a good ride and a good time. Had a talk with Charlie Abernathy in the store. (I am coming up to see you after Christmas.) (It is not too good for you.) (Haven't seen you for three years.) Saw Sam Carter. Saw Lena, and she went down street with me and rode to the crossing.

Friday, Dec. 13   Quite warm and pleasant. The wind blew pretty hard, though, and it grew more windy in the evening. I worked on the Christmas things for the babies. Walked down for the mail. Got a letter and magazine from Mr. Roberts. My chimney burned out today. Yesterday I got a chance to sell some more turnips and cabbages, so I guess none of them will spoil. Some people are very kind to me.

Saturday, Dec. 14   Very warm and very windy. About 4 o'clock it began to rain and just poured. I did up my work and worked on the babies Christmas things. I went down for the mail toward night when it was raining very hard and the walking was terrible. I got soaking wet. My feet were as wet as they could be. I fell down in a puddle too. When I got home I went right up stairs and put on dry clothes. Didn't go to bed until between 11 & 12. Baked bread between 10 & 11. Got a letter from Edith and a piece of music.

Sunday, Dec. 15   This morning the ground was covered with snow again, and it was colder. It kept growing colder all day and at night was real cold. I did up my work and took a bath and wrote two letters. Fixed one of those chickens that Aunt Laurinda dressed to cook and cut two of my fingers on my left hand.

Monday, Dec. 16   Pleasant and cold. I had a chicken dinner. Looked over a pan of pieces cut from newspapers and picked out some for Carroll's book. Toward night I drove up to the Mills with the mail. I didn't send it this morning because I thought Lula was going to Ogdensburg and I could send it by her. Curly rode up to the Mills with me. Sat up on the seat with the buffalo around him. I had a good ride. I sat up until 2 o'clock and worked on Carroll's book and kept the fire. It was a cold night.

Tuesday, Dec. 17   Pleasant and cold. I staid in all day and fussed around. Worked on the babies Christmas things in the evening. I felt tired and sleepy. I finished Carroll's scrap book. Kept fire and worked until 10 o'clock tonight. Didn't go down for the mail tonight.

Wednesday, Dec. 18   Pleasant and a little warmer. Bert got the mail. I got a letter from Mert. He has a good position and I am so glad and so glad to get his letter. I did up my work and worked on the babies books. Felt lonesome and sad and tired and sleepy. I sat up until about 12 o'clock keeping fire.

Thursday, Dec. 19   Warmer and storming. I got up in pretty good season and got my work all done up and started for Canton between 12 and 1. Came home by moonlight. I got the rest of my Christmas presents. Had a great time trying to decide on some of them. Had a fine ride all by myself. Got Mr. Roberts' letter and another big bundle of papers, two pictures and a piece of sheet music.

Friday, Dec. 20   Very pleasant. Bert and Lula went down town, and the baby staid with me. Grace Boyden came down and spent the afternoon with me. I finished Kathleen's book. I stopped my work to play games with Grace. I got so tired and nervous thinking of what I had to do tonight. Got Edith's letter that should have come Wednesday. Marvie drove in here on his way to Aunt Laurinda's.

Saturday, Dec. 21   Pleasant. Bert took Lula and the baby down to take the train for Ogdensburg.[76] Little Curly went to Canton too. I got my box of Christmas presents done up to send to Edith and Mr. R.'s present and Larnard's. About 4 o'clock I started for Canton to mail them. Drove back in the moonlight. My, but it was cold. The last mile and a half I put the lines around my neck. Got a letter from Mr. R. Aunt Laurinda and Marvie called here on their way back.

Sunday, Dec. 22   Pleasant but windy. I got supper last night for Bert and two meals today. Was busy most all day with housework. Wrote letters in the evening. Cooked the last two of those five chickens I had dressed. Took a bath in the afternoon.

Monday, Dec. 23   Pleasant. I did housework most all day. Got meals for Bert. Worked on little Maud's book in the evening. Got Edith's letter. I walked down for the mail just at night. I had chicken and biscuit for dinner.

Tuesday, Dec. 24   Pleasant. I did my work and finished Maud's picture book. Went down for the mail just at night. Got a Christmas present from Lena. I hurried around all day. Sent Mert's presents down to Carter's by Bert in the evening.

Wednesday, Dec. 25   Snowed until afternoon, then was lovely out. I got up early and got Bert's breakfast so he could go to Ogdensburg. I was alone all day. Mert came up to see me and staid a while but his time was so short he couldn't stay long. He brought me a bundle of presents. I went down for the mail and got packages of presents from Edith and Mr. R. and letters from both of them and a Christmas card from Aunt Mercy. I found presents from Bert and Lula on my plate this morning.

Thursday, Dec. 26   Pleasant. The boys went to the woods. I worked all day, mostly at housework. Got a paper from Edith with a pretty piece of music in it and a paper and two pictures and a piece of sheet music from Mr. Roberts. We played dominoes in the evening.

Friday, Dec. 27   Snowed in the forenoon but came off very pleasant in the afternoon. I did up my work and got dinner for the boys, then went over to Uncle Orson Wallace's funeral. I drove my own horse and Mr. Carter rode with me. When I came back I took care of my own horse for the boys had walked up to the woods back of the barn for something. Mr. Nichols spent the evening with me. I didn't get to bed very early.

Saturday, Dec. 28   Pleasant. I was late getting up and had lots to do. Mrs. Pitt came down in the afternoon. Mr. Pitt came after her and they staid in the evening a while. The two Misses Throope from Prescott were here also, walked down from Uncle Nelson's. Mr. Throope came after them and staid a little while. I got a letter from Mr. Roberts. I baked four big loaves of bread. Had a lot of dishes to wash after they all went home.

Sunday, Dec. 29   Rained or snowed most all day. Mr. Nichols helped me dress the potatoes for dinner and wiped the dishes. In the afternoon those young people came down again, were here to supper and in the evening. We had lots of music and a good time. (What Mr. Nichols said to me.) I didn't get to bed very early tonight either. I didn't get any chance to write my letters.

Monday, Dec. 30   Very pleasant. I did up my work and straightened things around in the forenoon. Aunt Mercy, Edith and Ethel came, were here to dinner, and in the afternoon they took me and we went up to Mr. Mott's. Saw the new twin babies. I rode down to the corner with them and got the mail. Got a letter from Edith. In the evening Mr. Nichols and I went down town. I got pretty cold. Washed my dinner and supper dishes after we got back. Mr. N. wiped the dishes.

Tuesday, Dec. 31   Blustering and cold. A bad day. The boys went to the woods. I wrote two letters and did up my work. It grew colder at night. The boys got the mail. I got a letter from Mabel Lewis. I staid up and kept a fire late or rather Mr. Nichols and I did. Well, good bye to 1901.

MEMORANDA

This little book must be put away now. Another year gone, another sad year for me, another great trouble in my life. Oh, such times. I wonder how I have lived through it all. I hope the next year will give me better days. Life can never be the same again without my precious mother and father but I will try for their dear sakes and with their lives as examples to do my very best. If I can only keep my dear home. It has been a hard struggle to try to do that. How much can happen in a year. How much has happened in my life in the last two years, joy and sorrow. The deepest sorrow has come to me twice and the greatest joy has come also. I thank God now for the dear ones that are left here and for the dear father and mother in heaven and that I had them here as long as I did.

1902. What will it mean to me? I hope it means good times. Now this book must be put away with the rest of my diaries, and I must start my new one.

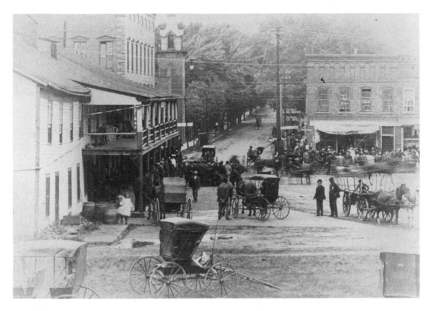

The America House corner, a central meeting place in Canton, N.Y., c. 1900

In this detail of a map of landowners of St. Lawrence County, the Wait farm is located on the second crossroad below Brick Chapel and is marked by the name "M. R. Wait." The names of many of the Wait neighbors are also noted. The village of Canton is five miles to the north.   © 1896 Edward G. Blankman

The Wait Farmhouse

Mabel Wait, Almeda Wait, Edith Wait, Marvin R. Wait,
unknown, and Merton Wait, c. 1896

⮞ 1902 ⮜

JANUARY

Wednesday, Jan. 1   Cold and pleasant. I did up my work and made cookies and a pudding for dinner and bread. It was just like any other day this year, no extra dinner or anything. I was tired and kind of lonesome. I walked down for the mail just at night. Got a letter from Mr. Roberts and a very pretty calendar and card. Got my "Ladies' Home Journal" and a letter for Papa. Mr. N. and I staid up to keep fires as it was a very cold night and watched the old year out and the new in. (What he said to me.) Guy came to get the cutter to go to the New Year's ball at Russell.

Thursday, Jan. 2   Warmer and not quite so pleasant. I did my work, made some ginger cake and a jell[y] cake and pared and stewed apples for sauce. The wind began to blow hard in the afternoon and grew worse until it was blowing real hard in the evening again. Mr. Nichols went for the mail after supper. I got a letter from Edith and one from the Universalist Publishing House. I went to bed about 8 o'clock and had a good night's rest.

Friday, Jan. 3   Colder again. I did up my work in good season and made two pies before dinner. The boys drove over to Mr. Wells after groceries. Bert went down after the mail after supper but all there was was a letter for Papa. It was cold and we staid up and kept fires later, that is Mr. Nichols and I did.

Saturday, Jan. 4   Pleasant and cold. I slicked up the house, did my Saturday's work. Got it done early and took a bath and changed my clothes. It was cold again and we kept fires again and had a talk. Oh dear, such times. The boys got the mail. I got a letter from Edith, such times as I do have. It beats all. Sometimes I get so tired of everything it seems as if I couldn't stand it.

Sunday, Jan. 5   Very pleasant. No, not so very either for it snowed quite a bit. We were real late getting around this morning, I suppose because we staid up so late last night. Had breakfast between 10 & 11 o'clock and dinner between 3 & 4, just the two meals. I wrote to

Edith and Mr. R. in the evening then went to bed about 8 o'clock. Had a fine night's sleep. Mr. Nichols wiped the dishes for me as he does every day, the meals that he can.

Monday, Jan. 6   Very pleasant. The boys went to the woods. I did up my work and made some ginger cookies. Missed the delivery rig this morning and we had a lot of letters to send. I was so sorry. ~~The boys went over to the shop in the afternoon and got the mail on the way back. I got a letter from Mr. R.~~ Didn't get to bed until later. Didn't get the mail today.

Tuesday, Jan. 7   Very pleasant. The boys went to the woods. I did up my work and played on the organ quite a while. Made a wine plant pie.[1] The boys got the mail when they went to the factory this morning. I got a letter from Mr. R. No mail in the afternoon. Didn't get to bed until late. Laid down a while in the afternoon.

Wednesday, Jan. 8   Pleasant. I did up the work and played on the organ quite a while in the forenoon. I walked down for the mail in the afternoon and enjoyed the walk. Got a letter from Edith and one from Mr. R. I got (mad) after dinner or felt badly over something the boys said. Went to bed about 11 o'clock.

Thursday, Jan. 9   Pleasant and mild. I did up my work. The boys went to the woods and got back early. I made some biscuit for supper and they were lovely. Walked down for the mail just at night, but there wasn't any. After supper and after we got the work done up Mr. Nichols and I drove up to the Mills. Had a fine ride as it was nice out. Didn't get to bed very early.

Friday, Jan. 10   Pleasant. I did up my work and all of my Saturday's work. Had it all done before dinner. I spent the afternoon talking to Mr. N. Then when they went to chores I ironed and made a cake, etc. and had supper ready when they came in. Didn't get to bed very early. Bert went after the mail after supper. I got a letter from Larnard and he said something at the end of his letter that did me lots of good.

Saturday, Jan. 11   Was real warm in the forenoon but grew colder and was quite cold at night. It snowed hard all day. I drove to Canton, started about 10:30 and got back about four. I took down the turnips and cabbage to Mr. Miller's folks and Mrs. Griffith. Staid quite a little while at Mrs. Griffith's and visited. I paid Mr. Conkey the interest on the note.[2] Saw Lena. I got a letter from Edith.

Sunday, Jan. 12   Snowed all day. I did my work and got the meals as usual. Had the toothache, it began just at night but grew better late in the evening. (My remedy for the toothache.) Didn't get to bed until late. I wrote to Edith and Mr. R. while the boys were doing the chores. Didn't see a team go by today.

Monday, Jan. 13   Snowed part of the time and grew colder. Was a pretty cold night. I made a pan of doughnuts. Went to bed about 11. Mr. N. says such good things to me. Mr. Nichols went after the mail. I got a letter from Mr. R. and it made me feel badly because I wrote something that's made him feel badly and he was so good about it. I cried at the supper table a little and the boys began to tell funny stories to cheer me up.

Tuesday, Jan. 14   Cold but pleasant. I did my work and washed a few clothes and baked bread. Didn't get to bed until late. I made some biscuit for dinner and they were fine. The boys cleaned all up in their part of the house and it looked very good. They washed, mopped etc. No mail today.

Wednesday, Jan. 15   Warmer and pleasant. Bert went to Ogdensburg, and Mr. Nichols and I kept house or rather are keeping house. I did my work up good and filled and washed all the lamps and lanterns, mine and theirs too. I made a couple of ginger cakes at supper time and they were fine. (What Mr. N. said to me.) I started to walk down for the mail just at night but the road was drifted so badly I backed out. Mr. N. went for it after supper but there wasn't any.

Thursday, Jan. 16   Pleasant and warm but snowed in the afternoon and grew colder at night. Mr. and Mrs. Gardner and Earl drove in to see me. They said Lena was expecting me down there today but I couldn't go, would like to though. Mr. N. went after the mail. I got letters from Edith, Carroll and Mr. R. and a paper from St. Louis and two pictures and a piece of sheet music. I wrote two letters while Charlie was doing the chores. We expected Bert's folks back today but they didn't come. We didn't go to bed until between 2 & 3 o'clock.

Friday, Jan. 17   Real cold. I missed the mail rig so couldn't send my letters. I did up my work and got our dinner. Then about 3 o'clock

Bert's folks came and I got dinner for them. They were all in here to supper, too. Mr. N. and I didn't go to bed very early tonight either. Such times. It is like a story. Why is it that I have so much love given me when I am not worth it?[3] Little Lou knew me all right. A beautiful moonlight night but cold.

Saturday, Jan. 18　　　Pleasant until evening when it stormed and the wind blew hard. I did up my work and swept and dusted up stairs and down. Ate breakfast with Bert's folks. A little after noon Aunt Laurinda and Marvie came. They ate dinner with me and staid until about 4 o'clock, then went up to Aunt Laurinda's house. Aunt Nellie sent me a hand stitched handkerchief and a little fancy paper parasol. I got letters from Edith and Mr. R. and Edith sent me a brick from Santa Claus's chimney. Mr. Nichols and I started to go down town in the evening but the roads were drifted something awful so we didn't go down there.

Sunday, Jan. 19　　　Very pleasant but cold and I suppose the roads are quite bad. I have seen a number of teams go by though. I did up my work and fussed around. Ate dinner with Bert's folks. Wrote to Edith and Mr. Roberts. Mr. Nichols came in here in the evening. We had a lunch of Johnny cake and milk that Lula brought in about 8 o'clock. Went to bed about 1 o'clock. A beautiful moonlight night. I sent my butter jar to the factory this morning.

Monday, Jan. 20　　　Very pleasant and some warmer. I did up my work and patched some. Made soup for dinner. Laid down and took a nap in the afternoon. Was sick in the evening but staid up. Mr. N. was in here. The boys went to the village in the afternoon. Another beautiful night.

Tuesday, Jan. 21　　　Snowed hard all day and in the night it turned to a rain and sleet and froze on and the wind blew hard. Mr. Nichols and I were going up to the Mills to a lecture but didn't on account of the weather. He spent the evening in here though. We played six games of dominoes in the fore part of the evening. I just did my common work. Laid down quite a while in the afternoon.

Wednesday, Jan. 22　　　Stormed most all day. I did my work and quite a bit of mending. The stage came this way and brought the mail. I got a letter from Edith and one from Eva in a letter to Bert. Wrote some letters in the evening. Mr. Nichols and I started to drive up to the Mills again in the evening, or rather got ready to go but it began to rain. I guess the weather is against us. We didn't go to bed until late.

Thursday, Jan. 23   Pleasant. Mr. N. went up to Uncle Nelson's to paint their kitchen. He got back about dusk. Bert went to the woods after a load of wood. I did my common work and a few extras. I laid down in the afternoon. (The baby and the pail of ashes.) Of course Mr. Nichols spent the evening with me. He went to bed about 11 o'clock. I set bread after 11 o'clock. The stage went this way this morning.

Friday, Jan. 24   Very pleasant. I did up my work and then mended. Baked four loaves of bread. Little Lou ate supper in here with me. Mr. N. went up to Uncle Nelson's again to help cut some wood. He got back quite early and brought the mail. I got a lovely large picture from Lena and a little note. We didn't go to bed until late. (Our topic of conversation the last two hours.)

Saturday, Jan. 25   Very pleasant. I did my common work and mended some. Wrote two letters in the afternoon. Little Lou came in to help me then so I didn't write any more but spent my time with her. Mr. Nichols went up to Uncle Nelson's to help them again today. He was kind of late getting back. He brought the mail and I got a letter from Edith and two from Mr. Roberts and my "Ladies' Home Journal." We didn't go to bed until about 3 o'clock.

Sunday, Jan. 26   It snowed and blew most all day. The wind blew hard all day anyway. Mr. N. and I were going over to Net's but didn't because the weather was bad. He was in to see me most all day. I wrote two letters just at night. We went to bed between 8 & 9 o'clock. I had a good night's sleep, about 10 hours. Ate dinner with Bert's folks.

Monday, Jan. 27   The wind blew hard all day. It was thawing and raining in the morning but grew colder all day and was a very cold night, as cold as we have had. The [wind] blew awful hard in the evening. I ate supper with Bert's folks. (All alone in the dark.) Mr. Nichols spent the evening with me and was in a while in the afternoon. Little Lou was in here most all day. I mended my black waist. Laid down a while in the afternoon.

Tuesday, Jan. 28   Pleasant and cold. A very cold night. I did my work and did some patching. Mr. N. was in here in the forenoon quite a while and in the evening. The baby was in here most all day.

Wednesday, Jan. 29   Cold and pleasant. Uncle Nelson came down in the forenoon and staid quite a while. I did up my work. Then Mr. N. and

I fixed the big chair, the back was loose. The baby was in here quite a lot. I walked down for the mail just at night. Got letters from Edith and Mr. Roberts, a St. Louis paper and the "Plaindealer." Mr. N. was in here in the evening. The boys went over to Little River and I sent for some groceries.

Thursday, Jan. 30   Quite pleasant but cold. The boys went to the woods. I did my work and then mended. Finished making over the two pairs of little stockings for the babies. I put my clothes to soak at night and got ready to wash. Mr. Nichols was in here in the afternoon a while and in the evening. Fred Hosley came over in the evening to see if I would go over there and help them a little as his wife isn't well and they have no girl.

Friday, Jan. 31   A lovely day. I did up just what work I had to in the morning and then walked over to Mr. Hosley's. I helped her all day, ironed some, sewed quite a lot and did some other odd jobs. I enjoyed the day, too. Mr. Nichols came over after me in the evening. I brought home a pair of pillow cases to make for Mabel Hosley. Mr. N. spent the evening in here. I got a letter from Mert. Was pretty glad to get it. It grew colder in the evening.

FEBRUARY

Saturday, Feb. 1   Quite pleasant and mild. Snowed quite a bit toward night. I did a big washing and got it all out on the line a little after noon. I ate dinner and supper with Bert's folks. In the evening Mr. Nichols and I went down town and went to the show only we didn't see any play for it was a failure. A big audience sat in the Opera House nearly an hour then we all went home.[4] I got letters from Edith and Mr. Roberts.

Sunday, Feb. 2   Snowed hard, the wind blew a hurricane and it drifted all day. At night it was awful. Mr. N. went out and got my clothes for me off from the line. He was in here most all day and in the evening. (Such an experience in the evening.)

Monday, Feb. 3   Stormed some and the wind blew all day. We were snowed in. No team went by, and there was no road to be seen. I did up my work and made one of Mrs. Hosley's pillow cases. Made a ginger cake. Mr. N. was in here most all day and in the evening. Went to bed in pretty good season and slept good.

Tuesday, Feb. 4   Very pleasant. The teams plowed out the roads and it looked more civilized again. I made Mrs. Hosley's other pillow case. Mr. N. was in here in the forenoon and a little while in the afternoon and in the evening. After supper we drove over to Mr. Hosley's with the pillow cases. Aunt Laurinda was there. We didn't go to bed very early.

Wednesday, Feb. 5   Pleasant. I did my common work. Mr. N. was in here part of the time in the day time and in the evening. He went after the mail. My letters didn't come today. I wrote to Edith and Mr. Roberts.

Thursday, Feb. 6   Very pleasant. Bert and Lula went to the village. Mr. Nichols and baby Lou ate dinner with me. I did up my work, the common work and some extras. Mr. N. was in here a good share of the day and in the evening. Bert and Lula went down for the mail after supper. I got letters from Edith, Mr. Roberts, and Larnard and each one of them had something in it to make me feel badly. If it hadn't been for Mr. N. I would have had an awful evening. I was pretty blue for a while as it was.

Friday, Feb. 7   Snowed some most all day. I did my common work. Mr. N. was in to see me most all the afternoon. In the evening he and I went down town to see "Pauline" the great mind reader and mystic. It was good. I saw Tom Carter in the post office. We had quite a cold stormy ride. When we got back the fire was all out. I built it up and we had some supper. Lula went down for the mail just at night. Little Lou was up stairs with me all the time while I was getting ready to go down town. I got a letter from James Thompson.

Saturday, Feb. 8   Stormy. Snowed some all day. I did my common work and swept and dusted. Laid down a while in the afternoon. No one went after the mail today. Lula made some candy, butterscotch. We went to bed about 11 o'clock, or I did for I took a bath after Mr. N. went.

Sunday, Feb. 9   Pleasant. They plowed out the road again. There was no road to be seen this morning. I just did up my work and then talked to Mr. N. Baby Lou was in here a good share of the time.

Monday, Feb. 10   Very pleasant. I did up my work and made some doughnuts. (Baby Lou and the sugar.) Mr. N. got Saturday's mail when he went to the factory this morning. I got a letter from Edith. I did my work and wrote to Edith, Mert, and Mr. Roberts. Mr. Nichols was in here in the evening and for a while in the day time. (I sent my butter jar this morning.)

Tuesday, Feb. 11   Very pleasant in the morning but it began to snow and blow and drift and toward night we had quite a blizzard. I did up my work. Had a headache and didn't feel well. I laid down on the lounge in the afternoon. Mr. and Mrs. Hobbs (Belle Nichols) and Mrs. Nichols came. Mr. N. was in to see me in the forenoon, afternoon and evening a little while. I was out there with all of them in the evening.

Wednesday, Feb. 12   Snowed some. I didn't do much today. Ate dinner with all of them out in the other part. They were in here some. Charlie was in to see me and was in here in the evening. Belle washed the dishes and I wiped them after dinner. I got a letter from Mr. Roberts. Lula made ice cream and brought me some ice cream and cake. We are all invited up to Uncle Nelson's to dinner tomorrow.

Thursday, Feb. 13   A lovely day. I did up my work and was going up to Uncle Nelson's with the rest of them but just as I was going to get ready Mrs. Billings came so I staid at home. She was here to dinner but didn't stay to supper. They were all in here in the evening. I had a fire in the parlor and they played and sang. Mr. N. staid "a while" after the rest went to bed. I got a letter from Edith and a pretty valentine from Mr. R. Lula and I went out to see the calves when the boys were milking. I got little Lou to sleep.

Friday, Feb. 14   Quite mild but snowed a little. Our company went home. They were all in here for a while. I ate dinner with them and was out there quite a lot. Helped Lula do up her work. A beautiful moonlight night. Bert and Lula went down for the mail after supper but there wasn't any. Charlie was in here in the evening.

Saturday, Feb. 15   Very pleasant, just fine out. I was sick. Felt real bad in the forenoon but not as bad in the afternoon. I laid down for a while. Couldn't do much work. Bert went to factory meeting in the afternoon and Lula and the baby went down to Carter's while he was there. I had a crying spell in the evening. Mr. N. was in here afternoon and evening. I got a beautiful valentine from Mert and a letter and roll of papers from Edith.

Sunday, Feb. 16   A beautiful day. I did up my work and got ready to go over to Net's. Mr. N. and I went, were there to dinner and all the afternoon. Had a lovely ride. We didn't get back until after dark. He was in here in the evening. Another lovely moonlight night.

Monday, Feb. 17   A pretty good day but it snowed some and the wind blew some. I felt kind of bad and sad. Had another crying spell. I wrote to Edith, Mert, and Mr. Roberts. Mr. Nichols was in here in the evening and some in the daytime.

Tuesday, Feb. 18   It snowed and blew and drifted today. We wanted to go down town to a play this evening but couldn't. Lula had one of her spells today. Such a time. Mr. N. was in to see me several times and in the evening.

Wednesday, Feb. 19   Pleasant. The men plowed out the roads. I did my work and did some mending. (My company to sew.) Bert went over to the store and I sent for some things. Mr. Nichols was in here in the afternoon and he and I went over to Mr. Billings in the evening. It was a beautiful moonlight night but real cold. No mail today. Mrs. Billings got supper for us in the evening.

Thursday, Feb. 20   Pleasant. I did my common work. Lula went after the mail in the evening. I got letters from Edith and Mr. Roberts and a St. Louis paper. Mr. Nichols was in to see me. Another lovely night.

Friday, Feb. 21   Very pleasant, just fine out. Bert and Lula went to the village, and Charlie and little Lou ate dinner with me. He was in here part of the forenoon and part of the afternoon. Toward night I swept the chambers. Wrote to Edith. In the evening Mr. N. and I went up to Aunt Laurinda's. It was a beautiful night.

Saturday, Feb. 22   A lovely day and night. I did my Saturday's work, swept and dusted the sitting rooms and mopped the oilcloths and dusted the chambers. I took a bath in the afternoon. No mail today. Mr. N. was sick today. He was in here in the evening. I felt sad today.

Sunday, Feb. 23   Another beautiful day. I did up my work. Mr. N. was in to see me in the forenoon. Bert and Lula and the baby went for a ride in the afternoon. Mr. N. was in here in the afternoon, too. I had another crying spell. In the evening we went up to the Mills to church. The people seemed glad to see us. I wrote to Edith and Mr. Roberts.

Monday, Feb. 24   A nice day until afternoon when it began to rain. I did my common work. Laid down in the afternoon. I felt kind of sick to my stomach. Looked over some beans and cooked them. Mr. N. was in to see me in the afternoon a while and in the evening. I got a letter from Edith.

Tuesday, Feb. 25   Very pleasant except it was foggy toward night. Just like spring out. I did my common work and made some cookies. Walked down for the mail just at night. Mr. N. was in here some in the forenoon, afternoon, and evening. I wanted to go somewhere, it was so nice, but didn't.

Wednesday, Feb. 26   A beautiful day, just like spring. I sat out on the porch a long time after dinner. This has been a sad day for me, so many things happened to make me feel badly. What Ira Bullis stopped here for made me feel badly, and Mr. N. and I had a little trouble and then something in my letters. I walked down for the mail in the afternoon. Got letters from Edith, Irma, Mr. Stiles, and from the Insurance Co. Just at night Anson Andrews called on me. I was surprised to see him for I didn't know he was at home. I had two or three crying spells today. Mr. N. didn't come in here until nearly chore time, then he came in the evening.

Thursday, Feb. 27   Another beautiful day. I did up my work, then Mr. Nichols and I went down town. Had a lovely ride. I called at Lee Wallace's and at Mr. Leighton's to see Aunt Mercy going down. We drove up to Lena's and talked with her quite a while, and she rode around the square with us. Coming home, little Maud was out there to Carter's and we stopped to see her. I got a good letter from Mr. Roberts. Mr. Nichols was in here all he could be today. I sent $5.75 to the Insurance Co. today and 10 cts. to send it.

Friday, Feb. 28   Pleasant in the morning, but toward night it began to rain, and the wind began to blow hard about noon. I wrote to Edith and Mr. R. While I was getting dinner, the chimney burned out. I was a little frightened for the boys were at the woods and Lula, the baby and I here, but it turned out to be all right. It was a wild night. Mr. Nichols was in here in the afternoon quite a while and in the evening. The milk was so thick they wouldn't take it at the factory so the boys had to churn it at home.

MARCH

Saturday, Mar. 1   Pleasant part of the time, and rained part of the time. I did my Saturday's work and talked with Mr. Nichols the rest of the time. The stage came this way. I got a paper from Mr. R. and one from Edith but my letters didn't come. Something happened in the evening that made me feel very badly. Mr. Nichols put some hinges on the storm door for me. He was in here as usual.

Sunday, Mar. 2   Rained hard all day long. I just did up my work, then talked with Mr. N. Ate dinner with Bert's folks. Wrote more letters just at night. Got weighed today and weighed 131 pounds. It rained all the evening, too. We went to bed about 11 o'clock.

Monday, Mar. 3   It snowed most all day and was some colder. Just did my common work in the daytime. I was going to write, but little Lou was in here and wouldn't let me do much of anything but I wrote one letter just before supper and then Mr. N. came in and spent the evening, and after he went to bed I wrote three more letters, so I have six ready to send. The mail rigs didn't go down today. I suppose the water is over the road down to the bridge. (How I went after the snow) (and got my feet soaking wet.) Baby Lou and I had some waxed sugar. The boys drew out manure.

Tuesday, Mar. 4   Pleasant and bright. I did my work and quite a lot of mending besides. No mail today. I was going out for a walk it was so pleasant but I finally didn't. Lula and the baby went for a walk and rode back on the manure wagon with the boys. Mr. N. was in here a while in the forenoon and in the evening. Bert went over to the store in the forenoon. I sent six letters this morning.

Wednesday, Mar. 5   Quite pleasant but the sun didn't shine and it was colder. I did up my work and did some more patching. Made an apple and a mince pie. The boys went to the woods in the forenoon. Mr. N. was in here in the afternoon and evening. I walked down for the mail in the afternoon. Got letters from Edith and Mr. Roberts. Wrote to them in the evening. Got a paper from St. Louis too.

Thursday, Mar. 6   Very pleasant. I did my work and baked four loaves of bread. I took a bath in the forenoon. Laid down a little while in the afternoon. Got a lovely big picture of Mert and nine of the students that he sent me. I was pretty glad to get it. I read some today.

Friday, Mar. 7   Rained some, then turned to snow. In the afternoon, Mr. Nichols and I went down town. It was snowing but was quite warm. Had a very pleasant ride. I paid the taxes and saw Mr. Morely about printing the poems. The taxes were $18.22. We had a sack of lovely chocolates. (Such an experience as we had in the evening.) Charlie and I played dominoes in the evening.

Saturday, Mar. 8　　　　Pleasant and quite a bit colder. When I woke up one side of my face was puffed right out, swollen from a hollow tooth. I suppose I took cold in it. I look very pretty with it. I did all my Saturday's work. Baby Lou was in here most all day. Mr. N. was in afternoon and evening. I got letters from Edith and Mr. Roberts. I copied the two poems for the "Plaindealer."

Sunday, Mar. 9　　　　Pleasant and warm but in the afternoon it rained and snowed some. My face was just the same today. I did up my work, read some, wrote some and spent the rest of my time with Mr. N. and baby Lou. I had two or three crying spells toward night.

Monday, Mar. 10　　　　A beautiful day. I did my common work and then did whatever I wanted to. Read a little while. Mr. N. was in here a while in the afternoon and in the evening. I laid down a while in the afternoon.

Tuesday, Mar. 11　　　　Very pleasant in the morning but began to rain in the afternoon and rained harder and the wind blew in the evening. Little Lou was in here about all day. She ate dinner with me. I made a ginger cake in the afternoon. Mr. N. went after the mail. I got a letter from Mr. Stiles and one from Irma that I didn't like a little bit. Mr. N. was in a while in the afternoon and in the evening. I sugared off in the evening and asked them in to eat it.

Wednesday, Mar. 12　　　　Rained in the forenoon but was just cloudy in the afternoon and was warm. It began to rain again in the night. The wind blew in the evening. I walked down for the mail but found the box empty. Mr. N. was in here a while in the forenoon, afternoon, and evening. I wrote to Edith. I read a little the fore part of the evening. Mr. N. and I played dominoes in the evening.

Thursday, Mar. 13　　　　It rained, then grew colder and snowed. I did up my work and looked over some beans and cooked them. I was late getting up this morning. I sewed on some hooks and eyes and buttons on some of my clothes. Mr. N. was in a while in the afternoon and evening. He went after the mail but there wasn't any today either. It is queer. New moon tonight.

Friday, Mar. 14   Very pleasant. I felt poorly all day long and felt so bad in the evening I had to go to bed early. I just did my common work. Mr. N. was in here more or less. When the boys went to the factory, they found the mail in the box. The stage driver must have put it there late yesterday afternoon. I got letters from Edith, Mr. R. and Larnard. Mr. and Mrs. Cole and their little girl called on me just at night. I was going out for a walk but didn't get started. I sent my butter jar this morning.

Saturday, Mar. 15   A beautiful day. I was sick and staid in bed until about one o'clock. About eleven Lula came up to see me and then brought me some toast, egg, and tea. (The old woman that stopped here.) After I got up I did my Saturday's work. Went for a little walk toward night. Lena, Mr. Hastings, Bessie Dies, and Mr. Ruggles came along in a double rig and Lena ran in to see me. Mr. N. was in here in the evening and just for a few minutes in the afternoon. I got letters from Edith and Mr. Roberts.

Sunday, Mar. 16   Rained in the morning and again toward night and the wind blew hard all day. Mr. N. was in here most all day and in the evening. I wrote my letters toward night.

Monday, Mar. 17   Pleasant and cold. I did my common work and fussed around. It was a lovely moonlight night. I went out in the other part of the house just about supper time and sat down to the table with them and talked a while. Mr. Nichols and I went for a walk in the evening down to the corner and back. He was in here a while at noon and in the evening.

Tuesday, Mar. 18   Pleasant and cold. I did my common work and started to sew a little but baby Lou was in here and wanted me to pay my attention to her. Bert and Lula went to the village in the afternoon. I didn't feel very well. Mr. N. was in here a while toward night. In the evening he and I went over to Ira Bullis and took her back home. We spent the evening and they sugared off for us. It was a lovely moonlight night.

Wednesday, Mar. 19   Cold, real cold. I did up my work and washed out a few clothes etc. In the afternoon Mr. Nichols and I went down town. I was quite cold when I got to Canton. Mr. N. came in here, staid until supper was ready when we got back. After supper Aunt Mercy came. Mr. Carter brought her up. I asked Bert's folks in here in the evening. Lula didn't come but the boys did. Aunt Mercy and I had a good talk. I heard that Tom Carter is married. Had a sack of lovely chocolates.

Thursday, Mar. 20   Pleasant in the morning but rained the rest of the day. I did up my work and got a pretty good dinner. In the afternoon I carried Aunt Mercy over to Net's. (How I paid Dolph for hitching the horse.) Little Lou was in here for a long time and ate dinner with us. Yesterday Mrs. Carter sent me a very cute picture of baby Maud. I was pleased with it.

Friday, Mar. 21   It rained part of the time and was pleasant part. Was nice in the evening, moonlight and warm. I did my common work and swept the sitting room all over for Saturday. Wrote a letter and sent it down by Mr. Pitt. Little Lou was in here a good share of the time. Mr. N. was in a few minutes at a time different times. In the evening he and I went up to Mr. Pitt's a while. They sugared off for us.

Saturday, Mar. 22   It rained in the morning but came off pleasant, was very pleasant toward night and in the evening. The boys took some veal calves down town in the forenoon. Mr. N. was in here quite a while after dinner. I dusted all over and did my common work. I walked down for the mail in the afternoon. Got a letter from Edith. Sat out on the porch quite a while when I got back. Mr. N. was in here a little while in the evening, but we went to bed early.

Sunday, Mar. 23   A beautiful day and a beautiful moonlight night. I did up my work and wrote some and read some in the forenoon. The boys went up to Bullis' sugar house. In the afternoon Mr. N. was in here a while then we went for a walk up to Boyden's and up on the cross road a piece. We sat down on the side of the road for a quite a while. Stopped in to Mr. Boyden's and had some sugar. I saw Mr. Hubbard. He came along while we were out walking.

Monday, Mar. 24   Very pleasant. I did a big washing. Had the line full. I was real tired. After doing the washing I swept and mopped up the oilcloths and cleaned up all of the wash things and emptied the waters. Then I sat up late in the evening, until 2 o'clock. Mr. N. was in here a little while in the morning, & afternoon and was in in the evening.

Tuesday, Mar. 25   Very pleasant. I did my work and did lots of little odd jobs. Mr. N. was in a while in the forenoon, afternoon, and evening. We are having beautiful moonlight nights all the time.

Wednesday, Mar. 26   Very pleasant. Mr. Nichols and I started for Norwood at 7 o'clock in the morning. Got to Uncle Ing's about ten, called, then went on to Marvie's. Stayed there to dinner and supper both, then drove on to Norwood. Saw Marvie's new baby. (The road we took to go to Norwood.) We had a pan of popcorn there at Ed's in the evening, and lots of music. Arthur Farmer was there. We had a lovely ride, it was so pleasant.

Thursday, Mar. 27   Pleasant most all day, began to rain toward night. In the morning Edie and I went over street. I wrote a postal and we made a call. Mr. N. was down street getting a shave and he walked back with us. We did up the work then Aunt Mercy, Edie, Mr. N. and I went up to Hat's to dinner. In the afternoon we all, and Hat too, went to call at Will Thompson's. Aunt Laurinda was there. We came home in the rain. Spent the evening at Ed's again.

Friday, Mar. 28   Very warm and pleasant. Mr. Nichols and I went for a walk around town in the forenoon, then sat out on the steps quite a while. He and I went over to the noon train to see Edie and Maud off. They went to Plum Brook. After dinner we started for home. Stopped at Uncle Ing's to supper and then came home. The roads from Norwood to Potsdam were just fine but from Potsdam home they were real muddy. I found quite a lot of mail waiting for me. Letters from Edith, Mert, and Mr. R. and a lot of papers. Charlie got some of the loveliest great big chocolates this morning.

Saturday, Mar. 29   It rained most all day. Mr. N. was in here quite a bit. We had a little trouble and I cried most all day. He was picking things to get ready to go home. It was a pretty sad day taking it all around. No one went after the mail.

Sunday, Mar. 30   Pleasant and colder. Mr. N. was in here most all day, and we didn't go to bed at all. Staid up until morning. The terrible crying spell. Uncle Ing walked out. He stopped here a while then went up to Uncle Nelson. I cooked a good dinner. It is Easter Sunday. Miltie Pitt came down and invited us up to eat warm sugar so Charlie and I took a walk up. We didn't get back until just dark. I ate supper with Bert's folks. Bert got the mail this morning when he went to the factory. I got a letter from Edith and cute little Easter cards from Edith, Carroll, Kathleen, and Helene.

Monday, Mar. 31   Quite cold in the forenoon and snowed a few flakes, but was fine in the afternoon. I didn't have to get up this morning. Had breakfast early. Haven't had any sleep today either. I wrote two letters this morning and sent them. In the afternoon Mr. N. and I went for a walk up to the woods and to the spring and clear up on Waterman's Hill. Had a nice walk. I found some may-flowers in the woods.

APRIL

Tuesday, Apr. 1   It was rather pleasant in the forenoon but rained in the afternoon hard. In the evening it turned to snow. Uncle Ing came down from Uncle Nelson's. He was in Bert's part of the house mostly. He went back just at night. Charlie was in here in the forenoon and a while toward night and we sat up all night. Charlie went after the mail but there wasn't any. It was a sad day for us for he was talking about going home. It snowed, hailed, and rained.

Wednesday, Apr. 2   It snowed all day long, was a damp, disagreeable day, and a sad day for me and for a very dear friend of mine. I didn't have to get up this morning, either. Charlie spent all the time he could with me. He started for Canton to take the train for home about 9:00. Oh, but I hated to have him go. We both cried. Bert got the mail down town. I got letters from Edith and Mr. R. I couldn't eat hardly a bit of breakfast or dinner. Had a crying spell after dinner. I went to bed at 7 o'clock.

Thursday, Apr. 3   Cold but quite pleasant. I did up my work then mended. I mended five or six pairs of stockings. Laid down a little while in the afternoon. I walked down for the mail but there wasn't any. Little Lou was in here most all the forenoon.

Friday, Apr. 4   Quite pleasant. Another long lonesome day for me. I did my work and then mended again. I walked down for the mail in the afternoon but got nothing but papers and I expected a letter. I could have cried. I felt more lonely than ever for I thought I would get a letter from Charlie today. I staid outdoors quite a while after supper. Read some too.

Saturday, Apr. 5   Very pleasant, just a beautiful day. And I was <u>so</u> lonesome. I did my Saturday's work and had it all done by noon. Just at noon Aunt Laurinda and Marvie came. They stayed until 3 o'clock. They ate dinner with Bert's folks. I walked down for the mail and got just exactly what I wanted. Letters from Edith, Mr. R., Charlie, and one from Mr. Cleaveland and the paper from Aunt Mercy.

Sunday, Apr. 6   A beautiful day. It couldn't be nicer. How I would liked to have gone for a walk, if I had only had the right one to go with. I wrote seven letters or finished them up. I partly wrote three last night and got three rolls of papers and a package done up ready to send. Guess I'll fill up some mail train tomorrow. I sat out on the porch quite a while three different times. Went for a little walk (Curly and I) just at dusk. Heard the church bell ring and the frogs and birds were singing and the ducks sailing around on the pond. Everything was so nice out and yet I was lonely, so lonely.

Monday, Apr. 7   Another beautiful day. I got my work done up and got ready early to go to town but Bert was using the horses so I waited until afternoon. Curly and I went for a walk in the forenoon and I went in to Mr. Pitt's a while. Had a good ride down town. Took care of my horse when I got back.

Tuesday, Apr. 8   Colder and very windy. In the morning I walked down to try and catch the stage to mail a letter but I was a little late for it and had to send my letter by the free delivery rig. I called on Mrs. Poole. I did quite a bit of mending today. Walked down for the mail just at night, Curly and I. Got a letter from Eva and she wants me to come out there right off.

Wednesday, Apr. 9   The wind blew a hurricane all day long and it rained some. I was very loncsome. I mended some and read some in "The Little Minister."[5] Little Lou was in here for quite a while with me this afternoon. Just at night I walked down for the mail. Got a letter from Edith. Little Curly went with me, as he does every time. Poor little Curly and I are pretty lonesome. In the evening I wrote Edith and Eva.

Thursday, Apr. 10   Cloudy and cold all day. It snowed a little just at night. I was sick. Staid up stairs most all day. Laid down part of the time and sat up part of the time. I finished reading "The Little Minister" and liked it very much. I walked down for the mail toward night. Got a letter and paper from Mr. Roberts.

Friday, Apr. 11   Very pleasant. I worked hard all day cleaning up in the sitting room and was very tired at night. Bert and Lula and the baby went down town in the afternoon. I got a letter from Mr. Nichols. (The young man enlarging pictures.) I thought I would go out somewhere in the afternoon it was so lovely but I didn't get around to it. I felt so lonesome and discouraged.

Saturday, Apr. 12   It was lovely in the morning but clouded up and we had an April shower after dinner then it was cloudy all the afternoon and the wind blew hard. I finished cleaning up the sitting room and bedrooms. Got my work all done about 3 o'clock, then I walked down for the mail. Got a letter from Edith. I laid down after I got back. Read some in the evening then went to bed.

Sunday, Apr. 13   It hailed two or three times hard, rained two or three times, and was pleasant part of the time. April weather surely. I did up my work, then little Lou came in here and I spent quite a while playing with her, then I slicked up and changed my clothes and got my dinner, then wrote to Edith and Mr. Nichols then read in "The Prince of the House of David." I was very lonesome as usual. This is Mert's birthday.

Monday, Apr. 14   Cold all day. Cloudy in the forenoon, but the sun shone in the afternoon. I did quite a lot of odd jobs in the forenoon. Little Lou was in to see me a while both forenoon and afternoon. I walked down for the mail in the afternoon and Aunt Laurinda was in to Mrs. Poole's and called me in. I made quite a call. The two Mrs. Bullises came to call too while I was there. Got a fine letter from Mr. Roberts. I heard that Irma had come home, came Saturday.

Tuesday, Apr. 15   A beautiful day. I worked all day, baked, ironed, swept and dusted the chambers etc. I didn't work all the time either for I played on the organ quite a bit. Bert and Lula and the baby drove to Ogdensburg and back. Didn't get back here until 9 o'clock. Mr. N. sent me a box full of lovely chocolates and a package of pepsin gum in it too. I was much pleased to think he remembered me so. I walked down for the mail but there wasn't any. Aunt Laurinda came up and staid all night with me.

Wednesday, Apr. 16   A beautiful day. I did up my work and changed my clothes and walked down to the cemetary, then I called on Lee Wallace and on the Misses Rodee. Staid quite a little while. Then called at the factory and got my mail and came home. Got a letter from Edith, and two from Carroll in it. I had a nice walk and heard quite a bit of news.

Thursday, Apr. 17   Very pleasant most all the time. It threatened rain once about 1 o'clock, but it didn't amount to anything but was real pleasant again. I did up my work and got ready to go down town if I could get there. I started out about 1 o'clock, called at Jessie Rodee's and at Mr. Leighton's. He was going down town a little later so I waited and rode with him. Got down there about 5 o'clock. Went up to Mrs. Griffith's to see about my waist, then did some shopping and went up to Mr. Gardner's to stay all night. Kittie and I went down street in the evening and she slept with me. Lena had a beau. I got a letter from Larnard.

Friday, Apr. 18 A beautiful day. Lena and I took an early morning walk over to the new cemetary, Fairview. I had never been over there before. When we came back we sat in the hotel sitting room and I waited for a chance to ride home. Mr. Wheeler was there. I went back up to Mr. Gardner's to dinner. Then went down street and finished up my shopping and rode home with Mr. Billings in a double wagon and walked from the corner by the schoolhouse and carried my parcels. I got a letter from Mr. Roberts and a package of papers. I was tired and went to bed early.

Saturday, Apr. 19 Very pleasant. I did up my Saturday's work, took a bath and slicked up and walked down for the mail. Got letters from Edith, Mr. Roberts and Eva. Bert and I had a great talk in the morning. I wrote a short letter to Mr. R. this morning. I read a little in the evening then went to bed. It thundered and lightened in the evening and rained a little.

Sunday, Apr. 20 Rained hard in the morning and was dark and gloomy, but it cleared off and was very pleasant. I wrote a long letter to Edith and read some. Mr. and Mrs. Griffith called on me in the afternoon. She fell in love with everything in this dear old home. She thought it so pleasant and so cozy and nice inside. Between 4 and 5 o'clock I started out for a walk. I asked Cora if she didn't want to go for a walk when I got up there and we finally walked up to the Mills to church. Milton came up and brought us home. Then Curly and I had our supper and I had to write my letter to Mr. Roberts and do several things.

Monday, Apr. 21 It was cloudy in the morning and toward noon began to rain. It rained hard all the afternoon. I did quite a few odd jobs today, fixing my clothes. I laid down in the afternoon. Bert went after the mail. I got a paper from Mert. Little Lou was in here a little while just at night. I brought water to fill the reservoir and boiler to be ready to wash in the morning. Read a little while in the evening and went to bed early.

Tuesday, Apr. 22 Pleasant and very warm but the wind blew hard all day. It was lovely just at night though when I walked down for the mail. I got a letter from Mr. Nichols and his picture. I did a great big washing today and carried so much water and everything that I am pretty tired tonight. Got my washing all done at 12 o'clock. I have got a sore arm tonight. I burned it this morning and then this afternoon rubbed off the blister so it is pretty sore. I did up papers to send to Edith, Mert, and Mr. R. and wrote a letter to Mr. N. in the evening.

Wednesday, Apr. 23   A queer day. This morning it was kind of cloudy then the wind began to blow hard and it rained a little then it was pleasant all day but very windy and toward night it grew cooler and was quite cool. I walked down to catch the stage this morning and waited in to Mrs. Poole's. I walked down for the mail this afternoon and found the box open and the mail blown all around. I went in to Mrs. Poole's a few minutes again to take Aunt Laurinda some paper and envelopes. I picked cowslips for some greens for dinner. The chimney burned out again at dinner time. Got a letter from Edith.

Thursday, Apr. 24   All kinds of weather today. This morning it was real pleasant but after a while it clouded up and rained some and snowed some. Then in the afternoon it was pleasant again. It was cold all day but in the evening began to grow warmer again. I did some mending and a number of things getting ready to go to Ogdensburg. I walked down for the mail in the afternoon. Got a letter from Mr. Roberts. Wrote to him in the evening.

Friday, Apr. 25   A beautiful day. Just right, neither too warm or too cold, and it is my dear father's birthday. I got my work done up early and was ready to go down town but had to wait around to see if Bert got the check. They were going down town too so Bert put both seats in the double buggy and we all went. I wrote a letter to Larnard and sent him $85. on the money we have of his. Paid ten cts. for registering the letter. I got my waist at Mrs. Griffith's. Got my dinner when I got back then walked down for the mail and stopped a little while to visit with Aunt Laurinda and Mrs. Poole. Aunt L. came home with me and staid all night.

Saturday, Apr. 26   It rained more or less all day, just poured part of the time and was pleasant part of the time. I did quite a big day's work and got it done early too and everything looked so neat and nice. In the afternoon I sewed some. Bert went down for the mail but it wasn't there. I am so sorry. Probably the stage driver didn't bring it because it rained so hard. Aunt Laurinda went home or down to Mrs. Poole's rather on the milk wagon.

Sunday, Apr. 27   Cold and cloudy and rained in the forenoon. Late in the afternoon it cleared off and was lovely out. Then Curly and I went for a walk and went over and saw Mrs. Hosley's new baby. I read most all day. Was very lonesome. Little Lou was in to see me a little while. Ed, Edith and Susie Mott called here this afternoon. I let them take Em's big picture to Aunt Mercy. I was so sorry not to have my letters to answer today.

Monday, Apr. 28   Very pleasant. I got my work all done up and everything ready to go to Ogdensburg. In the afternoon I walked down for the mail and found out Mr. and Mrs. Poole were going down town and I could ride with them so I went back and hurried around and got ready to start. Mr. Cole called on me just before I started. Mr. Poole drove up for me. After I got down town I wrote postals to Edith and Mr. Roberts. Took the 6:36 train for Ogdensburg. Had a real time getting down here. Saw Mr. N. as soon as I got off from the street car and he didn't know me. Got letters from Edith, Mr. Roberts and Larnard and the beautiful poem "Memories of Home" from Edith.

Tuesday, Apr. 29   A very pleasant day but toward night it clouded up and began to rain and rained hard. In the morning I walked up to school with Eva and back for a walk.[6] It is a mile and I had a lovely walk. Then I read quite a bit and wrote a letter to Mert. In the afternoon I went up to school and staid the afternoon. In the evening Eva and I went up street and back on the car. Just as we got back, Mr. N. came and spent the evening. Eva, Estace, Charlie and I played dominoes. (Out on the steps.)

Wednesday, Apr. 30   Kind of cloudy and dull in the forenoon, but pleasant in the afternoon. I got letters from Edith and Mr. R. and answered them in the forenoon. Wrote 20 pages in one and 15 in the other. Mr. R.'s letter was fine. In the afternoon I went up to school with Eva. In the evening Mr. Kennedy and Mr. Savage came up and spent the evening. About 11 o'clock we had cookies and coffee. We played dominoes. Eva and I had a great talk today and it made me feel very badly. She that was Minnie Nichols called after school and Marcia Martyn.

MAY

Thursday, May 1   Pleasant. Kind of cold in the morning. I went up to school with Eva in the forenoon. George Johnston called on me while I was gone. In the afternoon I read quite a bit. Eva got home early and we called at Mrs. Nichols then Eva, Anna, and I went down to the woods and got some flowers. Had a fine walk. Coming back we met Mr. Johnston and he stopped to speak to me. In the evening Mr. Kennedy, Mr. Johnston and Miss Burke were here.

Friday, May 2　　　　A lovely day. In the forenoon I went up to school with Eva and heard the Arbor Day exercises. We got back early. In the afternoon we went down to the Hospital, walked both ways. Had a fine walk. I got letters from Mr. Roberts and Mr. Stiles. We called at two houses on our way down to the Hospital. I got an introduction to a gentleman friend of Mr. Kennedy's, Mr. Martyn. In the evening Charlie and Anna Nichols were over. We played dominoes again. Mr. K. stopped here a while on his way up to Lodge.

Saturday, May 3　　　　Cloudy and cold and rained some. I staid in all day and read and fussed around. Got a letter from Edith. Wrote to Edith and Mr. Roberts. In the evening Mr. Kennedy and Eva, Mr. Savage and I went to the play "The Royal Box."[7] It was very good. (The fire.) I was a little bit lonesome today because I couldn't get out on account of its being so damp.

Sunday, May 4　　　　Rained some but was pleasant most of the time. In the morning we went to church and Mr. Nichols went with us. In the afternoon, the Odd Fellows went over to Prescott to church and Eva and I went. I met Mr. Coeval. Such a time with fellows today. We went to church in the evening, Eva, Estace, and I. Mr. K. was here to supper. Mr. Savage was to come but didn't. Perhaps he came after we went to church. After I got home from church I finished up my letters. Old Mr. Nichols came over after the milk this morning and came in to see me. George Johnston, Miss Burke and Miss Johnston called in the afternoon.

Monday, May 5　　　　Rained in the morning but came off pleasant and was a beautiful afternoon and evening. I finished my letters and took a bath then started to go up to Minnie Best's. I was going to walk but got a ride with some man. Staid there to dinner and supper. Eva came up after school. Minnie and the baby and I came down to meet her. Charlie Nichols was there both to dinner and supper. After supper we went for a ride. It was lovely out and I enjoyed the ride so much. I went back up street with him to leave the rig then we walked down. Got a St. Louis paper. Oh, such a lot of trouble.

Tuesday, May 6   A lovely day, but clouded up in the afternoon and began to rain about 11 o'clock at night. I walked up to school and back with Eva both forenoon and afternoon. Read some in the forenoon. George Johnston called in the forenoon. Jennie and I went to the woods in the afternoon. Mr. Savage called just before supper to see if we could go over to Prescott Thursday night. In the evening I went to a concert at the Presbyterian church with Charlie Nichols. I was sick just at night. Laid down a little while in the afternoon.

Wednesday, May 7   Windy and cold. I staid in all day until time for school to be out, then I walked up to meet Eva and she came another way so I walked back alone. I wrote to Edith and Mr. Roberts. Got a letter from Edith. George Johnston stopped to see me in the afternoon. In the evening Eva and I went up to choir practice and Mr. Kennedy and Mr. Coeval came home with us and spent the evening. We had supper about 10 o'clock. I like Mr. Coeval pretty well.

Thursday, May 8   Pleasant until toward night when it began to rain. I laid down a while, in the forenoon finished the handkerchief I was working on, and Jennie and I took a walk down to the river. In the afternoon George Johnston called again. (What he said.) Minnie Best and the baby were here to supper. In the evening Mr. Kennedy and Mr. Savage were here. We were going over to Prescott but it rained so we didn't. It thundered and lightened hard too. We played dominoes. Mr. Savage and I had some games of dominoes by ourselves afterward. I got a letter and paper from Mr. Roberts.

Friday, May 9   Very cold and very windy. I staid in the house all day. Read quite a bit. George Johnston stopped to see me. I laid down in the afternoon and went to sleep. Frances Smith came home with Eva and was here to supper and in the evening. Charlie Nichols came over and spent the evening. We played dominoes. (Our talk.) Got a letter and a paper from Mr. Roberts.

Saturday, May 10   Pleasant and cold. Eva washed and I washed out my clothes. George Johnston stopped to see me. I wrote to Edith and Mr. Roberts. Laid down in the afternoon and had a nap. In the evening Charlie Nichols and I went up to Minnie's and spent the evening. Had a pleasant time. Eva said Mr. Savage came up to see me after I had gone. (Out on the steps.) Edith's letter didn't come. I was so sorry.

Sunday, May 11   Very pleasant and warmer. Eva and I went to the Universalist church in the forenoon. We walked both ways. We staid in the house all the afternoon and read some. I laid down a little while. In the evening Mr. Nichols and I went to the Methodist church. We took a walk afterward.

Monday, May 12   Pleasant but quite a cool wind. I laid down in the forenoon. I was so sleepy and had quite a nap. (My caller.) Got a letter from Edith. Mr. Johnston stopped to see me in the forenoon and came up in the evening. In the afternoon Jennie and I took a long walk down to the Hospital grounds and river and all around. I saw Mr. Cole and Archie and Willie.

Tuesday, May 13   Pleasant. In the morning I walked up a piece with Eva, as far as the bridge. I worked on one of my handkerchiefs part of the day. Laid down a little while in the afternoon. Walked up to school and sat on the steps until school was out. In the evening Mr. Savage came up and spent the evening with me. (Out on the steps.) He is getting woke up so I like him pretty well.

Wednesday, May 14   Pleasant. In the morning I walked up a piece with Eva. Took a bath after I got back and laid down a little while before dinner. In the afternoon I walked a little way with Eva then Jennie and I went for a walk. We went down by the woods this side of the Hospital and met George Johnston and rode back with him clear up to Greene St. In the evening Mr. N. and I went down to Mr. Hobbs. We rode as far as the street car goes going down and walked a mile and walked all the way back. (Our talk.)

Thursday, May 15   Pleasant. I finished writing to Edith (started the letter yesterday) and wrote to Mr. Roberts. I walked up to school and back with Eva in the morning. Walked up a piece with Eva in the afternoon too. I sat out doors in the afternoon in the warm sunshine. Anna Nichols and I walked up to meet Eva at night. We started once and were too early and rode back with Estace on the sand wagon then we walked back to meet Eva again. Eva went to choir practice in the evening. I walked down to the corner with her and Mr. Savage came along and talked quite a while with me. George Johnston spent the evening with me. (Our talk.) Got a letter from Edith.

Friday, May 16   Pleasant. I laid down and slept most all of the forenoon. Got a letter and paper from Mr. Roberts. In the afternoon Jennie and I went for a walk down on the bank of the river. I picked up a lot of shells. I sat out on the steps the rest of the afternoon. Mr. Johnston called on his way down to the Hospital. In the evening Mr. N. and I went to the reception at the Presbyterian church for the new minister. The orchestra played all the evening, and they served ice cream cake and strawberries. We stopped at Minnie Best's. It was a lovely evening.

Saturday, May 17   A beautiful day. I kind of rested all day for I was very tired. I laid down both in the forenoon and afternoon. I wrote to Edith in the afternoon. Marcia Martyn was over in the afternoon. In the evening Mr. Savage and I went to the Opera "Floradora."[8] It was fine. I like him better the more I get acquainted with him. Such a crowd on the street car going up. (Who I saw.) Got a letter from Edith.

Sunday, May 18   A beautiful day. Eva and I went to church in the forenoon and walked both ways. The sun was awful hot. In the afternoon Mr. Nichols and I went for a boat ride. It was fine on the water. We went about three miles down the river and landed on Chimney Island and sat there quite a while under the trees. Had a sack of oranges and bananas. Started for home between 5 & 6. Ate supper then we went to church over to the Congregationalist church. A lovely night. We went for a little walk after we got back from church and sat out on the steps a long time. (Our talk.) The patient.

Monday, May 19   Pleasant. I wrote most all the forenoon. Laid down in the afternoon and slept until school was out. Marcia Martyn came over for a while toward night. I had a night off and went to bed early. I felt sad. Such a mixed up mess. I guess I won't have as many callers after this. Got a letter from Edith and Mr. Roberts. Mr. Kennedy was up to see Eva and Mr. Haley to see Jennie in the evening. I went to bed. Walked up a piece with Eva in the morning.

Tuesday, May 20   Very pleasant. I walked up a piece with Eva in the morning. Worked on my handkerchief most all the afternoon. Did a little of everything and not much of anything today. Maggie and Nellie Johnston came over to supper and staid in the evening. We played dominoes. (Charlie came over after the milk.)

Wednesday, May 21   Pleasant. I walked up with Eva in the morning and we got to talking and had a regular "fight" in talk, but it came out all right. Jennie and I sat out on the steps the rest of the forenoon. I got letters from Bert and Mabel Lewis. In the afternoon I went up to school with

Eva and staid during the afternoon. Charlie Nichols spent the evening with me. We went for a walk. A lovely night.

Thursday, May 22   Pleasant and hot, kind of windy and dusty too. I walked up with Eva in the morning. Stopped and talked with Anna when I came back. Sat out on the steps nearly all the time. Right after dinner Jennie and I sat out under the trees. (The fight we saw.) In the afternoon I took a bath and cleaned all up, and felt better. After supper Marcia Martyn, Eva, and I walked up to her sister's Mrs. Goodno, and back. John was up to see Eva. I went to bed about 9 o'clock. It began to rain soon after I came up stairs and rained hard. I wrote to Edith in the forenoon.

Friday, May 23   Pleasant. I walked up with Eva in the morning. It was very warm today. Jennie and I had a pitcher of lemonade. I wrote a letter to Bert. Went over to Mrs. Nichols and talked with Anna quite a while. George Johnston came along, and I rode home with him and we had quite a talk. Got a letter and paper and picture from Mr. Roberts, a fine letter. I slicked up in the afternoon and sat out on the steps. Laid down a few minutes. Marcia Martyn and Miss White came over while Jennie and I were both up stairs. Miss Stowley called. Charlie came over in the evening. We went for a walk. It began to rain before he went home and rained hard.

Saturday, May 24   Pleasant part of the time, and rained part of the time. Eva and I went up street in the forenoon. We walked up and rode back with George Johnston. He came in a few minutes twice. I washed and ironed my white waist or Eva washed it and some of her clothes and I ironed all of them. Such a time as I had ironing that waist. Got a letter from Edith. Eva and I went to bed early.

Sunday, May 25   Pleasant. Eva and I went to church in the forenoon. I had company to sit with me, Mr. Hobbs. I did my writing in the afternoon. Mr. Kennedy and Mr. Johnston were here a while in the afternoon and sat out on the steps with us. In the evening I went to church with Mr. Nichols. We went to the Presbyterian church. It was packed full. The Military Companies were there in a body. Out on the steps after church. When I went to church I took my letters along and put them in the mailbox.

Monday, May 26   When I woke up it was raining but it cleared off and was a fine day where we were. I got up about 4:30 and got ready to go on the Excursion to Kingston. It started at 7 o'clock. Roy Johnston and

Anna Nichols, Charlie Nichols and I went together. There was a very big crowd. It was a 160 mile trip. Took us 7 hrs. to go each way. Anna took a basket full of lunches for all of us. We had most everything to eat all day. I saw some beautiful scenery. Charlie got me some souvenirs of Kingston and the Islands. We got home between 1 & 2 o'clock. Came down in a hack.

Tuesday, May 27   Cloudy and cold. It rained some, showers every once in a while in the forenoon. Was quite pleasant in the afternoon. I slept until between 9 & 10 o'clock. Eva and I were invited up to Frances Smith's to supper. I went up to school about recess time. We walked around town quite a bit before we went to her house as Eva wanted to do some trading. Had a pleasant time at her house looking at her brother's collection of curios gathered from all parts of the world. We staid until about 8:30, then came home on the car. I had kind of a headache and felt kind of bad.

Wednesday, May 28   Very cold and dull. It rained a little and snowed a very little. I kept kind of quiet today for I didn't feel so very good. Mr. Johnston stopped a little while in the evening. Mr. N. came over to see me, Mr. Kennedy to see Eva and Mr. Haley to see Jennie. It was comical. I laid down a little while in the forenoon.

Thursday, May 29   Cold and cloudy. It grew some warmer toward night. I wrote letters to Edith and Mr. Roberts. I didn't feel extra good. Laid down a while. I was all alone part of the afternoon. Jennie went up street. I read. Anna Nichols and Bertha Adams were in a little while. Eva and I were going down to the Hospital to the Patients' dance in the evening but they didn't have any. George Johnston stopped in to tell us there wasn't any. Eva and I walked up street after supper and she bought some lilies-of-the valley for her mother's grave. We were out in a big wind storm. Stopped at Mrs. Goodno's. Got a letter and paper from Mr. R.

Friday, May 30   Very pleasant. I took a bath in the forenoon and got ready to go to Decoration Day. I went over and talked with Anna a little while in the morning, and staid outdoors quite a while. In the afternoon Eva and I went out to the cemetary on the street car and carried the flowers. We walked back and went to the Opera House to hear the address. Then we walked back to the cemetary with the crowd and walked clear back home. I was tired. There was a big crowd. The soldiers looked very nice marching. We stopped at Mrs. Goodno's coming back and rested a while. In the evening we went up to Uncle William's.

Saturday, May 31   Pleasant and warm. I didn't feel good at all. Was taken sick in the night and put in a great time. I laid down in the forenoon. In the afternoon kind of late, I changed my clothes. Eva and I laid out under the trees quite a while after dinner. John Kennedy stopped twice toward night. Charlie came over in the evening, and we went up to Minnie Best's. They had quite a bit of baby company there during the evening.

JUNE

Sunday, June 1   Pleasant. I was tired and didn't feel extra fine today. Eva and I went to church in the morning. We all sat out in the yard in the afternoon and watched the people. In the evening Charlie and I went to the Methodist church to hear a lady speak on Temperance. Five churches were united in the service. When we got back from church, we sat out on the steps and it was quite "early" when I went to bed.

Monday, June 2   Quite pleasant, rained a little bit once or twice. I got up early and got ready to come home. Called at Mr. Nichols to say good bye to them and bid all of Uncle John's folks good bye and went up to Minnie Best's as she and John Nichols were coming out too to see Lula. Charlie came over there and came to the train with us. We had to wait a while in DeKalb and had to wait two hours in Canton for the stage. I was tired. My Dear Old Home looked pretty good to me. I ate dinner and supper with Bert's folks. Staid out doors all the rest of the afternoon talking to John. He and I went for a walk in the evening.

Tuesday, June 3   Pleasant all day until just at night when it rained. I did quite a bit of work in the forenoon. In the afternoon Bert, John, Minnie, little Lou and I walked up to the spring. I sat out doors the rest of the afternoon. Walked down for the mail toward night but there wasn't any. Minnie came in to my part for a while and looked at the pictures. I sent my butter jar this morning.

Wednesday, June 4   It rained most all day. Cleared off at night and there was a pretty sunset. I did quite a bit of work in the forenoon. Laid down in the afternoon and had a nap. Minnie and the baby came in and staid quite a while with me. We had a big visit. I walked down for the mail and got three letters from Edith that had been to Canton, Ogd., and back to Canton again and one letter from Mr. Roberts. Tyler Martyn brought me the registered letter that Bert sent, this morning. I wrote letters to Edith and Mr. R.

Thursday, June 5   Pleasant. I got my work done up early and sat out on the porch for a long time waiting for the mail rig to come and take my letters. Mr. Cole called on me. John Nichols put on the screen door for me. He was in here quite a while visiting with me and looking at the pictures. I walked down for the mail in the afternoon but all I got was a letter for Lula. Lula and Minnie and the children went up to Uncle Nelson's in the afternoon to call. I sewed a little and read some in the evening.

Friday, June 6   Pleasant. I got up early and it was a good thing I did for Lula was taken sick. We put in a great day. I had Minnie's baby in here all day and little Lou the most of the time too. John staid in here the most of the time. I helped get dinner out there and do the dishes and ate dinner out there because Minnie would make me do it. They had Mrs. Carter here and Mrs. Robinson. Bert went after Aunt Laurinda, but she wouldn't come. I carried Minnie, John, and the baby down to take the 6:36 train but we were three min. late so they had to come back and stay over night. They ate supper with me and slept in my part, of course. Lula's baby was born about 11 o'clock.[9]

Saturday, June 7   It rained all the forenoon, but cleared off in the afternoon. Oh, but I am sick and tired and discouraged. Such times. Minnie and John took the stage down this morning. I walked down to the factory with them and we went in to Mrs. Poole's to wait. I came back home before the stage came as there was no one here but Bert's folks. They all ate breakfast in my part, Bert and Lou too. I had little Lou to take care of part of the time today and dressed her this morning. I had quite a lot of work to do today. Laid down about noon and had a nap. Walked down for the mail in the afternoon. Got letters from Edith and Mr. Roberts. I went up to see Lula and the new baby this afternoon.

Sunday, June 8   It rained most all day hard. I did up my work, wrote five letters and read some. Took a bath in the forenoon and slicked up. Went up and staid with Lula a while toward night and undressed little Lou. I was lonely but not as much as I would have been if I hadn't written so many letters.

Monday, June 9   Very pleasant. I did up my work and then mended. Two young men came along, one was enlarging pictures and talked with me quite a while. Little Lou was in here part of the time. Mrs. Carter came down to see Lula in the afternoon and she and I did up the work out there. She came in to my part before she went home. I walked down for the mail and got letters from Mr. Nichols and Aunt Mercy. Answered them in the evening.

Tuesday, June 10   It rained hard in the morning but cleared off in the afternoon. I did up my work and finished mending my stockings and washed out a few clothes that I wanted clean the last of the week. Little Lou was in here part of the time. Mr. Poole on the grocery cart came along and I sold him 18 doz. eggs. I laid down a little while in the afternoon. Walked down for the mail just at night but there wasn't any.

Wednesday, June 11   Pleasant all day, it sprinkled a little just about dark. I did up my work and then went out and washed all the dirty dishes in the other part of the house. Carrie Bullis and the children drove into the yard and talked with me quite a few minutes this forenoon. I fussed around and did odd little things in the afternoon. Walked down for the mail in the afternoon and talked with Mrs. Poole a few minutes. My letters didn't come, just the "Plaindealer." Went up and talked with Lula a while.

Thursday, June 12   It must have rained about all night last night and was cloudy and rainy early this morning but it cleared off and was a pleasant day. Aunt Louise called here early this morning to see Lula and the baby. She was in here a few minutes. I made some cookies today and swept and dusted the parlor. I laid down a while in the afternoon and had quite a nap. Walked down for the mail toward night and got letters from Edith and Minnie Best.

Friday, June 13   Cloudy in the morning but came off pleasant. I swept and dusted the chambers and sitting room and bedrooms. Changed my dress just long enough to go down for the mail. Just got two papers and no letters. I didn't feel well at all. Went to bed quite a while before dark, had a pain in my stomach and a headache and ached all over. Just after I had come up stairs Mert, Irma, and the baby drove in and talked a while but they didn't come into the house.

Saturday, June 14   Very pleasant and very warm. I finished slicking up the house and took a bath before noon, but I hurried. I baked bread and beans and a cake. Soon after dinner Mert drove in and talked with me quite a while. I was so glad to see him. He left Irma and the baby out here as the baby wasn't very well. I looked for Charlie most all the afternoon and evening, but he didn't come. I was disappointed. Walked down for the mail but there wasn't any. I didn't feel very well today either. Charlie did come just after I got into bed. I got up and got supper for him then we didn't go to bed at all. I was so glad to see him.

Sunday, June 15   Pleasant and very warm. Charlie and I both laid down toward morning this morning and between 6 & 7 o'clock I got up and got breakfast. He ate with me in here. We washed the dishes and I did up the work, then we had the time all to ourselves. We walked up to Boyden's Creek and sat on the stones quite a while. We ate dinner with Bert's folks. They wanted us to. Uncle Nelson and Aunt Louise called just at night. Charlie drove home in the night by moonlight when it was cooler. He started from the house between 11 & 12. I rode with him across the brook and we got to talking and had a great talk there in the road. I am glad we had that talk. I went to bed at 2 o'clock.

Monday, June 16   Pleasant in the morning but very warm. I got up at 8 o'clock. It was so warm and so late I didn't build any fire for breakfast but ate cold victuals. I laid down at 10 and slept until 2, then a big storm came up and woke me up. How it did rain for a while. I put down some of the windows and let Curly in then went back to sleep and slept until 5 o'clock. Then I ate another meal and walked down for the mail but there wasn't any. Little Lou ate both meals with me. I went to bed at 8 o'clock.

Tuesday, June 17   Pleasant and quite cool. I didn't get up until about 8 again. Did up my work, then sorted over old papers and cut out what I wanted to save from them. The men went to work on the road today. I laid down a while in the afternoon and had a good sleep. Walked down for the mail and got a letter from Edith. I went for a walk up in the pasture and found a few strawberries.

Wednesday, June 18   Very pleasant. I got up at 5 o'clock and did a good sized washing. I had to carry all the water, bring in wood etc. and empty all the dirty waters. I got the washing all done at noon but had to do up my work and clean up everything and put it away afterward so it was 2 o'clock before I was all through then I was pretty tired and laid down and slept until 5 o'clock or slept and rested. I walked down for the mail and got a letter and a roll of papers from Edith. I am wondering why Mr. R. doesn't write.

Thursday, June 19   Pleasant. I did up my work and starched my fine clothes then looked over old papers and cut out what I wanted to keep. In the afternoon I walked down to the cemetary. The weeping willows and rose bushes look fine and one rose bush is full of buds. I called at Lee Wallace's and staid quite a little while. I staid out doors the most of the time after I got home until it got cool then I came in and read a little and went to bed.

Friday, June 20   Very pleasant. I did up my work and then washed my hair. I went down in the meadow on the bridge to dry it in the sun and wind and little Lou came down there and staid with me. Had my hair all done by noon and it felt and looked better. Just at noon Marvie, Fannie, and the baby came. They staid here until between 3 & 4 o'clock then went up to Aunt Laurinda's. I laid down a little while after they went then walked down for the mail then I sat out on the porch and mended three pairs of stockings then read some. Went to bed early. Sent my butter jar this morning.

Saturday, June 21   It was raining hard in the morning and rained most all day but late in the afternoon it cleared off and the sun shone out pleasant. I did up my work and washed out my combs and hair brush then I sewed carpet rags. In the afternoon I laid down for quite a while then walked down for the mail. Got a letter from Edith and the baby's picture and a picture of Carroll and Kathleen taken out in the flower garden last summer. Little Helene Mabel is very sweet. I took a bath and put on clean clothes just before supper.

Sunday, June 22   Pleasant but windy and real cold. I did up my work then read "The Wrestler of Philippi"[10] all through. It is one of the books that Edith sent me last Xmas. It was interesting. I wrote to Edith last night and wrote some more today. I was very lonesome and sad and nervous today. Little Curly staid right with me most all day and kept me company.

Monday, June 23   Quite pleasant. We had two or three little showers but the sun shone most of the time. It was real cool. I did up my work and sewed a lot of carpet rags. Just about noon I popped a little corn, a basin full. I walked down for the mail but there wasn't any. Oh, I wonder what is the matter with Mr. Roberts that he doesn't write. I am getting so nervous over it. Little Lou and I went strawberrying down on the side of the road. We got a few. Three teams came along, people that I knew, and talked to me.

Tuesday, June 24   Pleasant in the morning but in the afternoon we had some very big showers. It just poured right down and thundered and lightened. I ironed in the forenoon after I got my work done up. In the afternoon I sorted over old papers. Just at night I walked down for the mail and got a letter from Charlie. My, but it was awful walking. I went to bed before dark or before it was dark enough to light a lamp.

Wednesday, June 25   Pleasant all day. I was sick, began to feel sick about 9:30 and felt worse later. I did up my work and managed to iron my two fine white skirts that I had sprinkled but I didn't feel much like it. I baked bread too. Spent quite a bit of my time on the bed after I got my work done. About 5 o'clock I washed up and changed my clothes and walked down for the mail. Got a letter from Edith and a copy of the verses she wrote for Aunt Mercy on Uncle Allen's death. They are fine. Little Lou ate breakfast with me and was in here quite a while twice.

Thursday, June 26   It must have rained all night last night by the looks of things this morning, but it was pleasant today only this afternoon the wind blew hard and we had a little shower just at night. I didn't feel very well today and laid down a good share of the day. I didn't wake up this morning until 9 o'clock. I walked down for the mail about 5 o'clock and got a roll of papers and box of flowers from Mr. Roberts. Oh, I am so glad that he is all right. The box had 3 doz. beautiful carnations in it and some ferns.

Friday, June 27   Pleasant part of the time and rained part of the time. I did up my work and did all of my Saturday's work, sweeping, dusting, and mopping etc. After dinner I laid down a while then got up and dressed and walked down for the mail. Got a great big box of candy from Mr. Roberts. I had only been back a little while when Jim McMinn drove into the yard. My, but I was surprised. He came in and staid between 3 & 4 hours and we had that talk that I have wanted to have for over 5 yrs. Oh, I am so glad. We never really knew each other before.

Saturday, June 28   A very pleasant day. I did up my work and changed my clothes and got ready to go down to the cemetary and take my carnations. Bert went to the village with some calves and I rode down with him and walked back. I found our lot all mowed when I got down there. I think Mr. Drury did it. It was very kind of him. The flowers looked very pretty when I got them fixed. I read quite a bit this afternoon. Had a headache all day and felt worried and lonesome. Didn't get any letters today. I staid out doors for a long time toward night and had little Lou and Curly for company. We went for walks, sat on the steps etc. and had a good time.

Sunday, June 29   Pleasant and cool. I did up my work and changed my clothes and spent the day reading, thinking, and looking at the books of famous paintings. Oh, I was lonesome and sad. Lots of teams went past here today riding out, or the people were, and how I did want a ride today too. I kept thinking and thinking today. I have such a complicated mess of thoughts. Oh, if things would ever get straightened out again in my life. I dread everything.

Monday, June 30   Pleasant in the morning. I did up my work and got ready and started for Canton afoot. I walked about halfway when a man from Morley came along and gave me a ride the rest of the way. I paid Mr. Conkey the interest and did some trading. In the afternoon it began to rain and rained hard. I rode home with Mr. Mott and walked from the corner in the mud and rain. Got letters from Edith and Mr. Roberts. Got down there just as the noon train was going and I suppose Jim went on it but I didn't see him. Saw she that was Effie Sheets and her little boy.

JULY

Tuesday, July 1   A beautiful day. I sponged and pressed and brushed my black suit after I got the work done up. Had a nice little dinner all by myself. A little short cake for dinner. Laid down a while in the afternoon then walked down for the mail but didn't find any. Aunt Laurinda was at Mrs. Poole's so I stopped in there for quite a while and visited. When I got back I took a pail and went all over the meadow looking for strawberries. Just got enough for supper. Went to bed early.

Wednesday, July 2   A beautiful day. I was kind of lazy and enjoyed myself today. Looked over my last year's diary to find out something I wanted to know. Took a bath in the forenoon and put on all clean clothes. Laid down a while in the afternoon then walked down for the mail. Went in to Mrs. Poole's on an errand and Mrs. Poole and Aunt Laurinda wanted me to stay to supper so I staid. I enjoyed my visit with them. Got letters from Edith, Mr. Stiles, and Charlie. Charlie said something fine in his letter. I wrote two letters in the evening.

Thursday, July 3   It was raining hard in the morning and rained all the forenoon but didn't in the afternoon. I felt kind of poorly all day. Started to try that sample of medicine that Mrs. Hosley gave me today. I laid down a little while in the forenoon and about two hours in the afternoon. Slept in the afternoon. Bert got the mail in the afternoon but there was none for me. I walked down to Mrs. Poole's and got the package of Banner Oats and the lemons that I asked her to get for me from the grocery wagon today.

Friday, July 4   Very warm and pleasant. I staid at home all day and was very lonesome. Uncle John and Eva came this morning to see Bert's folks. Eva came in here a few minutes to see me in the afternoon. I partly wrote a letter to Aunt Susan today, was writing it when they came. Had a letter ready to send to Charlie but didn't see the free delivery rig go by at all today. I walked down for the mail this afternoon but there wasn't any. Oh, but I am lonesome tonight and sad.

Saturday, July 5   Pleasant and very warm in the forenoon, rained some in the afternoon. I staid at home all day lonesome as ever except that I walked down for the mail in the afternoon then it wasn't there and I was so disappointed, and in the morning I walked down to send two letters by the stage and walked up to Ira Bullis to wait for it. Bert and Lula went to the village in the forenoon and Eva took care of the children. I went out there and talked a while with her, then little Lou came in here and staid. They all went up to Uncle Nelson's in the afternoon and Eva and Uncle John staid all night.

Sunday, July 6   Pleasant and warm. Uncle John and Eva came back and were in here to dinner and little Lou too, and the most of the forenoon. After they went home (they started about 1 o'clock) I did up my work and then wrote my letters. How I wished I could go for a ride or do something. I get so lonesome. Went to bed early.

Monday, July 7   Pleasant in the morning but clouded up and rained very hard. I was very lonesome. Read quite a little bit and did odd little jobs. Laid down twice. Little Lou brought in an orange to me this morning. I walked down for the mail toward night and got letters from Edith and Minnie Best. Minnie wants me to come out and stay two or three weeks with her. Some parts of Edith's letter made me cry as it was sad but it was a good letter. Mrs. Bullis brought along two papers that were left in their box Saturday, two of our papers.

Tuesday, July 8   Pleasant and very warm. I did up my work and then worked on the crazy work for my sofa pillow. Did quite a bit of work on it. Laid down on the floor in the parlor in the afternoon and went to sleep. Toward night I walked down for the mail but the box was empty. Then I walked up to Mr. Pitt's and staid quite a little while. Ate some new beets and wiped the dishes. They gave me a lot of beautiful pansies. In the evening some fellow went by and I was sitting at the table fixing my flowers and he said "Hello, Mabel."

Wednesday, July 9   Pleasant and warm. I did up my work and walked down to Mrs. Poole's to wait for the stage this morning as I wanted to send down for some fruit by him. Then I came back and did some more work and laid down a little while. After dinner I read a little then walked down for the mail. Got a letter from Mr. Roberts that made me feel badly and three papers and three very pretty pictures with them from him and a lovely souvenir of Ogdensburg from Charlie and the "Plaindealer." I wrote to Edith and Mr. R. in the afternoon.

Thursday, July 10   Very pleasant, an ideal day. I did up my work this morning and laid down a while. Then I had my dinner and changed my clothes and started to go down to the cemetary and carry some of the pansies and go in time to catch the stage man and pay him for bringing up that parcel. I stopped in to Mrs. Poole's and he was going to the village and she to the aid society so they said I could ride. I did and went clear to the village. Had a fine ride. We started back a little after 6 o'clock. Saw Zuar and talked with him quite a while and saw R. Barber and walked up the street with him. How it ended. I got letters from Edith and Aunt Mercy.

Friday, July 11   A beautiful day. I didn't have my work quite done up when Cora Pitt came along going down town. She waited for me and I got ready and went down with her. We got back about 1 o'clock. I had a nice ride. In the afternoon I swept up stairs and down. Then changed my clothes and walked down for the mail. Got a letter from Mr. Roberts.

Saturday, July 12   Another beautiful day. I did quite a bit of work. Put up two quart jars of wine plant[10] just in water. It was quite a job to get it ready. Baked bread. Cooked all the rest of the turnips to have to feed to Curly as they don't taste very good. Cooked a dinner, a few little potatoes I found under the bin and baked yams. Dusted the sitting room, parlor, and bedrooms, mopped the oilcloths and porch and big stone etc. About 3 o'clock I had my work all done and laid down until about 5, then took a bath and walked over to Mabel Hosley's and got some of that medicine and got the mail. Got a letter from Edith. Curly went with me, then we had our supper when we got back.

Sunday, July 13   Very pleasant. I did up my work, changed my clothes and wrote three letters, to Edith, Mr. Roberts and Minnie Best. Made a little cake this morning out of almost nothing and it was real good. I ate a big dinner but it was just new bread and butter and celery and cake and part of an orange but I was hungry and it tasted good. I read most all the afternoon. Went for a little walk just at night up in the pasture. How I did want to go for a ride but of course couldn't.

Monday, July 14   Very warm and pleasant until toward night when it thundered, lightened, and rained hard. I just did up my work and sewed all the buttons on my new waist and fussed around and thought and read, and built "Castles in the Air." But there is no use of my building "Castles" for everything works against me. Mrs. Boyden was up in their lot raking hay, and she came down and called on me. I walked down for the mail and got a letter from Mr. Roberts that made me feel very badly. I wonder if I will ever be happy again in this world. I wrote to Mr. R. in the evening. Oh, I wish I knew what to do.

Tuesday, July 15   When I first got up about 5 o'clock it was pleasant but it soon began to thunder, lighten and rain, and it made a business of all three. It was a terrible storm. Then it staid pleasant until about 5 o'clock in the afternoon when the performance was repeated. I laid down in the forenoon after I got my work done up. I felt so discouraged and bad. Then I sewed for over three hours. Mame Bullis and little Raymond came over looking for some of their turkeys. I brought quite a bit of water from the brook toward night. Walked down for the mail and got some of those papers and pictures from Mr. R.

Wednesday, July 16   A beautiful day, all day. I got up early and washed. Had quite a big washing and had it all done before noon. Then after dinner I cleaned up everything and put the house in order. Then I laid down a while and then changed my clothes and walked down for the mail. Got letters from Edith and Charlie. I brought in my clothes and put them away and did my work for the night then wrote to Edith. Charlie sent a little picture in his letter. The new doctor from the Mills was in Bert's part today.

Thursday, July 17   Kind of cloudy and looked like rain all day, but didn't rain and just at night it was real pleasant. I did up my work and changed my clothes and walked over to Mrs. Billings. Staid to dinner and supper and after supper Earl brought me home. Had a nice visit. Had my letter all ready to send to Edith but the mail rig went by while I was changing my clothes so I couldn't send it. Looked in the box for mail on my way home but didn't find any. Mrs. Billings gave me a cake of sugar, some gooseberries, and some currants to bring home. Sent my butter jar this morning.

Friday, July 18   Very pleasant. I did my common work and looked over and canned my currants and gooseberries and ironed my five waists and some handkerchiefs, napkins and pillow cases. In the afternoon I laid down for over an hour and went to sleep. A lady came along selling some linament and I bought a bottle. Walked down for the mail in the afternoon. I sat out on the steps and read a while toward night and had little Lou and Curly for company, then we went for a walk up the road and then clear up in the pasture nearly to the woods. Had a nice walk.

Saturday, July 19   Pleasant until between 3 & 4 o'clock when it began to rain. It didn't rain very hard. I got my work done up early and was going to try and get down town but finally gave it up. I sat down in the parlor in the afternoon and went to sleep in my chair. Walked down for the mail and talked with Mrs. Poole a few minutes. Got a letter from Mr. Roberts that I was so glad to get. It made me cry though for part of it was sad. I read it over three or four times. Edith's letter didn't come today. I went to bed early. Played on the organ quite a while just before dark.

Sunday, July 20   Rained some in the morning and forenoon but was pleasant most all day. I did up my work and changed my clothes then wrote to Mr. R., Edith, and Aunt Mercy. Before I got the last letter finished I was so sick I couldn't sit up and had to build a fire and get something hot. Such a time as I had. I laid down until about 6 o'clock then ate some toast and coffee and went to bed.

Monday, July 21   Pleasant part of the time and rained part of the time. I did up my work and then laid down in the forenoon. I didn't feel like moving around much. Read some. Walked down for the mail in the afternoon and got letters from Edith and Charlie. They were both good letters. I sat in the parlor toward night and looked at some of the pretty souvenirs and other things I have. I enjoy looking at them so much. Then I spent my time thinking how I would like to have things in the future.

Tuesday, July 22   Pleasant. I did up my work in the forenoon and brought water and filled up everything and then slicked up. Tried on my new waist. After dinner I walked over to Mrs. Hosley's and paid her that dollar then went to Mrs. Bullis' and spent the afternoon. Came home just before dark. Rode with some man to the corner. Mrs. Bullis gave me some green peas and some beets. The children, Hosley children and Nellie Boyden, gave me some flowers, so I had a lovely bouquet.

Wednesday, July 23   Very pleasant, just a beautiful day. I got up early and did up my work, and I was glad I did for about 8 o'clock Cora Pitt drove down and asked me if I didn't want to go berrying. Of course I did, so we went. We drove up to Mr. Northrup's and got Jennie and we drove clear up Pierpont way somewhere and wandered around some but there were no berries up there so we came back, down back of Mr. Pitt's woods, Cora and I, and picked berries there. We got between 5 & 6 qts. apiece. Jennie didn't come, she stopped at home. We had a fine ride way up country and saw lots of wild scenery. Met Dr. Ladd way up there. I got a letter from Edith. My, but I was awful tired at night and got sunburned and scratched but I enjoyed it. We took a lunch.

Thursday, July 24   It rained some and was pleasant some. I canned my berries this morning, looked them all over last night and was most awful tired. I had good luck canning them. I cooked some of my green peas for dinner. They tasted good. I laid down twice for a little while, I just ached all over. We did lots of walking yesterday. In the afternoon I walked down for the mail. Got one of the St. Louis papers and pictures, and Mert's Foresters paper. The back of my neck is real sore today where it was burned in the sun yesterday. I had my shirtwaist turned in at the neck. I wrote letters to Edith and Charlie in the evening. We had quite a thunder shower just at night.

Friday, July 25   Pleasant. I did all of my Saturday's work, sweeping, dusting, mopping etc. I also baked bread and had splendid luck with it. After I got the rest of my work done, I washed two of the milk pails (they hadn't been washed of course) and brought water and filled up everything. About 3 o'clock I was all through and took a bath and laid down for about 2 hours then I dressed and went down for the mail. Got a fine letter from Mr. Roberts and my "Ladies' Home Journal." Now I understand Mr. R. I guess. I went to bed early.

Saturday, July 26   Pleasant and very warm. I did up my work early and changed my clothes and wanted to see a chance to ride down town if I could as there were several things I needed but I saw no chance. I read some and fussed around. I kept nice and cool in the parlor if it was a warm day. In the afternoon I wrote to Mr. Roberts and copied Edith's poem "Memories of Home" for him. Walked down for the mail in the afternoon and got a letter from Edith. Carrie Bullis and little Elburn came over in the afternoon to see Lula's baby and talked with me a few minutes.

Sunday, July 27   Kind of cloudy and cool in the morning, but it came off as warm as ever and the sun shone. I did up my work (Curly had two meals today, one about 9 o'clock and the other about 3 o'clock) and then wrote to Edith and did a little other writing and then read. Just at night little Lou, Curly and I went for a walk and then sat on a stone back of the barn for a long time. Lou didn't want to come in when it was dark. I was lonesome today as usual and wished I could go for a ride as usual, and had to stay at home alone as usual.

Monday, July 28   Pleasant. I did up my work early and got ready so if I saw a chance to ride down town I could go but I saw no chance. I fussed around and read some. It is hard these days to settle my mind on any particular thing when everything is upside down so I do little odd jobs. I laid down in the afternoon, but it was so warm there wasn't much pleasure in it. Walked down for the mail and got a letter from Mr. Stiles. Just at night I went for a walk up in the pasture and sat on a rock by one of the little brooks and heard it ripple along and watched the sunset. Saw that Bert was working Dol with two shoes off and it made me feel very angry.

Tuesday, July 29   Pleasant and very warm. I did up my work, and just as I was thinking about starting my dinner Aunt Mercy and Net drove in. They staid until 5 o'clock and Net would have staid until about dark and Aunt Mercy all night only Dolph came over and said Ethel was sick so they went home. I was disappointed for I wanted Aunt Mercy to stay. I asked Lula and the children to come in, in the afternoon. I walked down for the mail just at night, and sat out on that stone by the mail box and talked with Mrs. Poole for a long time. She was sitting on the steps. Got a letter from Charlie. He is coming out the last of the week or first of next.

Wednesday, July 30   Pleasant and very warm. I didn't feel very good and couldn't settle my mind on anything nowadays anyway. I read some and laid down a while in the afternoon. Walked down for the mail in the afternoon and got a letter from Edith. Rode part way back with Dolly Boyden. Louise Wallace came along with the two little fresh air girls, and I went out to see them and to ask how Lee was. Edith told about getting a letter from Aunt Louise and what she said and it makes me so angry.[11] Wrote to Edith in the evening.

Thursday, July 31   Pleasant and very warm. In the afternoon Grace Boyden came down to see me and staid until most dark then I helped her drive the turkeys home and she gave me a lovely big bouquet of sweet peas. I called at Mr. Pitt's a few minutes and Mrs. P. gave me some double hollyhocks, so I have some lovely flowers. Grace gave me some pinks too. Grace and I walked down for the mail toward night and I got a letter from Aunt Mercy telling how little Ethel was hurt. In the forenoon I walked down to Mrs. Poole's to try and be there when the grocery cart came along and get some lemons etc. but it had just gone when I got there. I had a good visit. Little Lou was kind of sick just at night.

AUGUST

Friday, Aug. 1   Pleasant in the morning but turned out to be a rainy day. Bert had quite a lot of hay out to get wet. He has great times with his help in haying. It rained very hard in the afternoon. In the forenoon I did all of my Saturday's work. Got through at 1 o'clock. I had some new potatoes for dinner today. Cooked them with those in the other part and Lula brought in a piece of meat and a piece of custard pie for my dinner. In the afternoon I laid down. Walked down for the mail toward night. Got a letter from Charlie saying he would be out tomorrow. Got a letter for Papa.

Saturday, Aug. 2   Rained some and was pleasant some. I did up my work and took a bath and changed my clothes, then I laid down a while. In the afternoon I walked down for the mail and got a letter from Edith. Mrs. Carter came down and called in the afternoon. She staid here quite a while and asked me to ride over to Net's with her tomorrow. Lula started to go down and meet Charlie but only got a little ways and met him coming up with a livery rig. He came in to see me almost as soon as he got here, and staid. I was so glad to see him for he is so good to me. Charlie and I drove up to the Mills after supper. I ate supper out there.

Sunday, Aug. 3   Pleasant only we had a shower in the afternoon. I did up my work, then talked with Charlie. Between 10 & 11 o'clock Mert walked in. He and Irma and the baby drove out before daylight and were up to Mr. Carter's. He came down to tell me that they wanted me to come up there to dinner so I went and we took Charlie along. In the afternoon Mrs. Carter, baby Maud, and I drove over to Net's. Edie and Arthur Farmer were there and Aunt Mercy. When we got back Mert hitched up and he and Charlie and I came home and they were here to supper with me. Edie and Arthur came along and stopped for a while. Charlie was in here in the evening. I had a very pleasant day out of it. Had a good time with little Maud. Charlie brought me some bananas and chocolates.

Monday, Aug. 4   Very pleasant, a beautiful day. I didn't have breakfast very early for we don't get [a] very long night's sleep when he is here. In the afternoon Charlie and I went to the village, and I got a lot of groceries. We drove over to Dolph's on our way back and talked with them a few minutes. I had such a lovely ride and enjoyed it so much. Charlie got some oranges and we ate them on the road. Didn't get home until dark. I got a fine letter from Mr. Roberts. Saw Mrs. Gillette down town and talked with her a while and several other people.

Tuesday, Aug. 5   Pleasant. I just spent my time with Charlie. We staid in the house all day until in the evening when we walked down for the mail but there wasn't any. We had a walk though. Grace and Walter Boyden came down for the turkeys just at night, right in the yard here, and Grace called me out to see her ring she got [for] her birthday.

Wednesday, Aug. 6   Pleasant. I talked with Charlie until afternoon then we took a walk up to the spring in the woods. We sat there a while and enjoyed the scenery and talked then came back home. He got ready to go home and Lula and the children were going with him but she didn't get ready in time and that clock out there was slow and when they were ready to start it was nearly train time. Lula had an awful time over it for she was bound to go anyway. Charlie got the mail. I got a St. Louis paper and several other papers, and there was another letter for Papa. Charlie ate supper with me.

Thursday, Aug. 7   It was cool and cloudy in the morning and rained a little bit but not enough to amount to anything. I got up at 4:15 and got breakfast and got ready to take Charlie down to the early train. Had a nice ride down there. We were on time, and did everything up in good shape. When I got back home I did up my work and swept and dusted, etc. I fixed that "Quine" to take. I was tired and sleepy but didn't have much time to lie down. I did for a little while between 3 & 4 o'clock. I walked down for the mail and got a letter and paper from Edith and some more verses she wrote, "My Little Helpers," and they are fine as all of her verses are. I wrote letters in the evening. I am so lonesome.

Friday, Aug. 8   Kind of cool and cloudy in the morning. I was late getting around. Didn't have Mr. R.'s letter ready to send and had to hurry to get Edith's directed. I did up my work, baked bread, made a pan of doughnuts, baked beans etc. Worked most all day. I walked down for the mail in the afternoon and got a letter from Mabel Lewis. I was very angry over something that they did here but didn't say anything. Grace and Walter Boyden came down after the turkeys and talked with me a while. Grace wanted to look at my pictures that came with the St. Louis papers, and take some of the papers home to read. (How I came near getting caught!) It came off warm and pleasant.

Saturday, Aug. 9   Very pleasant. I walked down to the factory in the morning to send some mail by the stage. Went into Mrs. Poole's and sat down, she wasn't there but came in a little while. I talked quite a while with her. Bert's folks went to Ogdensburg. I staid alone all night but didn't even get nervous this time. Curly is lots of company. I walked down for the mail in the afternoon. Curly and I went for a walk just at night. It seemed so good not to hear so much hollering and all kinds of racket and trouble out in the other part of the house. Bert got Mr. Crossman to do the chores. Took my butter jar down to the factory.

Sunday, Aug. 10   Pleasant and warm in the forenoon but began to rain in the afternoon and rained hard. I got up early and got my breakfast and got my work done up. Then I laid down a while in the forenoon before changing my dress. I read quite a bit, played on the organ, went for a walk, and wrote. I was lonesome. Bert got back a little before 5 o'clock. I went to bed early.

Monday, Aug. 11   Rained more or less all day. I did up my work and did a lot of patching. Laid down a while in the afternoon. Walked down for the mail toward night and got a letter from Edith. Mrs. Carter drove over just at night to tell me how Irma tried to get over here but had to go home at last without coming. Bert and Mr. Crossman went to the village and were gone all the afternoon, so I was alone.

Tuesday, Aug. 12   Very pleasant, a beautiful day. I got up quite early and did my washing. Had it all done before noon. Laid down a while in the afternoon. Then changed my clothes and went down for the mail. Got a letter from Charlie. I took a walk around just at night. How beautiful everything looked. Oh, how I wish I felt as peaceful myself as everything looks. I went to bed early.

Wednesday, Aug. 13   Very pleasant. I did up my work, mopped the oilcloths, porch, and big stone, took a bath all before dinner. I ate an awful big dinner. Laid down a few minutes in the forenoon and about two hours in the afternoon and went to sleep. Then I changed my clothes and walked down for the mail. Got a letter from Edith and a fair book and the "Plaindealer." I wrote to Edith, Mr. Stiles and started a letter to Charlie. It was a beautiful day and night and I wanted to go somewhere but didn't.

Thursday, Aug. 14   Very pleasant. I did up my work, and then changed my clothes. Walked down for the mail in the afternoon, but there wasn't any. I felt very lonely and thought I would drive down town and get someone to come home with me. So between 4 & 5 o'clock after Bert got through using the horses I started for Canton. When I was going down Brick Chapel hill the buggy broke down. I got out and unhitched Dol and pulled the buggy out of the way and went back and got Tom Carter to fix it. I called on Mrs. Gillette, walked down street with Charlie Gillette, did my trading and then got Lena to come home with me. Walked down street with Kittie. Saw Zuar and talked with him. Lena and I had a lovely moonlight ride home. Didn't get home until after 10 o'clock.

Friday, Aug. 15   Rained some in the morning but came off very pleasant. Lena and I had a nice breakfast and I asked Bert to come in and eat with us and he did. I did up my work and finished my letter to Charlie. (Lena's and my scheme.) We had a nice dinner and both of us ate a very big dinner. Then I changed my clothes and toward night I carried Lena home. Got a letter from Edith. I had another nice ride. Took care of my horse both last night and tonight in the dark. I wouldn't let Lena go to sleep last night until most 1 o'clock. I kept talking to her. I had supper at Mrs. Gillette's last night. Edith's letter made me feel awful bad. Poor girl.

Saturday, Aug. 16   Pleasant part of the time and rained part of the time. I worked all the forenoon and part of the afternoon then was sick and had to go and lie down. I swept and washed the parlor windows outside and in and brought in wood and water etc. I was awful sick for a little while. Bert went to the village with a calf. Just at night I walked down for the mail and got a nice letter from Mr. Roberts and the St. Louis paper and Mert's "Farm and Home." I read a little in the evening but went to bed in good season. It was a beautiful moonlight night.

Sunday, Aug. 17   Pleasant the most of the time but we had two or three little showers. I did up my work and laid down a while then changed my clothes. In the afternoon I wrote a long letter to Edith and another long one to Mr. Roberts. I felt poorly all day. Read some. Went to bed in pretty good season.

Monday, Aug. 18   Very pleasant. I did up my work and did my small ironing and baked a ginger cake etc. Laid down in the afternoon and rested a while then got up and got ready to go down after Lena. Drove down just at night. Kittie rode down street with me and Lena rode back. (How Fred horse stood still in front of the meat market.) Lena and I had another lovely moonlight ride home and another great talk. Got a letter from Charlie and he sent me one of those pretty ties with my initial on it. He hadn't got my letter and it kind of worried me.

Tuesday, Aug. 19   Rained a little in the morning, but came off very pleasant. Two men from Howe's came up to fix the dining room roof. Uncle Ing came down from Mr. Carter's before Lena and I had finished breakfast. There were six of us to dinner for I asked Bert in to eat dinner too. The men were all here to supper too. Lena and I read some in the afternoon. We didn't go to bed until about 12 o'clock. We sat out on the porch in the moonlight and had some company. We had a great talk afterward. We walked down for the mail late.

Wednesday, Aug. 20   A very pleasant day. Lena and I didn't get up very early. We did up the work and fussed around some and fixed the little egg to send to Robert for his birthday. We also read some and played on the organ some. In the afternoon we took a quilt and two pillows out under the trees and laid there and enjoyed ourselves. We walked down for the mail and I got letters from Mr. R. and Charlie. Edith's letter didn't come and I am worried for fear she is sick. We had solid comfort all by ourselves and lots of fun.

Thursday, Aug. 21   We had an awful thunder shower early in the morning. It was cloudy some in the forenoon but came off pleasant in the afternoon. Lena and I staid in bed until 9 o'clock. Had breakfast about 10. Before we had eaten our breakfast Dr. Ladd and another man called to ask where Bert was. About 11 o'clock Mert and Ed drove in and asked if I wanted company for dinner. After dinner we went to the funeral. Lena and I went with them. We rode four in a carriage. Had a great ride. We went to Lee Wallace's funeral. I got a letter from Edith. Wrote three letters after we got home.

Friday, Aug. 22　　　Kind of pleasant. Cloudy part of the time and rained a little. In the morning Lena and I walked down with five letters and a roll of papers to send by the stage and walked up to Mabel Hosley's so Lena could get a sample of that medicine. Then I swept and dusted etc. after we got back. I didn't feel very well. Laid down a few minutes after dinner and went to sleep. Then I changed my clothes and we walked down for the mail then up to Mr. Pitt's. Cora wasn't at home so we didn't stay long. We sat out on the porch quite a while after supper and went to bed early. Got a letter from Mr. Roberts.

Saturday, Aug. 23　　　Pleasant the most of the time. Had a little shower or so in the forenoon, but was pleasant all of the afternoon. I did up my work and made some soup for dinner and baked beans etc. Lena and I didn't get up very early. In the afternoon, we drove up to Josie's and spent the afternoon. Had a pleasant visit. Got home about dark and drove down to the mailbox. Got a letter from Edith. She has been sick. I hope she will be better. We went to bed quite early tonight. Sent my butter jar this morning.

Sunday, Aug. 24　　　Very pleasant. We didn't get up until quite late. I did up the work and we got on a blue streak and just sat around. We had a great time trying to decide whether I would carry Lena home today or tomorrow but finally planned it for tomorrow morning. In the afternoon we walked clear over to Little River and sat there on the rocks quite a while. On our way back we found a lot of blackberries on the side of the road, and we ate a lot of them or I did. Mrs. Carter gave us some apples. We had supper when we got home and I wrote to Edith and Mr. R. and done up Helene's shoes ready to send.

Monday, Aug. 25　　　Very pleasant. We got up early and had break-fast, then started for Canton. Had a pleasant early ride. I drove around and got a few things and then drove right back. Got my "Ladies' Home Journal." In the afternoon I laid down and went to sleep. Sarah Rodee called getting money for fixing up the cemetary. I walked down for the mail and got a letter from Charlie. It made me feel sad. I sat out on the porch and read a while after supper. Went to bed in pretty good season. I feel lonely tonight.

Tuesday, Aug. 26   Pleasant. I did up my work and did some other things I had to do then I laid down a while in the forenoon and afternoon too and went to sleep. Then I changed my clothes and went for the mail. Got a letter from Lena. I mended my stockings (three pairs). Mr. Gardner's whole family came along coming from Pierpont and Lena came in to see me a few minutes. I read a little in the evening and went to bed early.

Wednesday, Aug. 27   Very pleasant. Just as I got my work done up this morning Bert came in and said he was going down town to the show and that I could ride down if I wanted to so I hurried and got ready. I went up to Lena's to dinner then she and I went to the show. Such a crowd. Most everybody and their cousins were there I guess. We had a great time getting in. I got so tired and disgusted over it. (The pretty little fellow with the blue eyes.) Saw Zuar. Got a letter from Edith.

Thursday, Aug. 28   Very pleasant. I did up my work and washed what dirty clothes I had and put them out on the grass. In the afternoon I swept and dusted in the parlor and parlor bedroom. Before I was through the Misses Rodee came to spend the afternoon. We had a good visit. I unhitched and hitched up their horse for them. Walked down for the mail just at night but there wasn't any. Mr. Crossman stopped to see if he could rent the farm another year, next year I mean.

Friday, Aug. 29   Very pleasant and very warm. I wrote a letter to Charlie this morning and sent it. Did up my work and swept, dusted, and mopped up the oilcloths and steps and made up the parlor bed etc. I brought in quite a lot of water too. Got my work all done at 2 o'clock and was tired. I laid down and staid until 5 o'clock. Then I took a bath, changed my clothes and walked down for the mail. Got a letter from Mr. R. and two St. Louis papers and pictures. When I was going for the mail, I met Dolly Boyden and rode back with her to the corner.

Saturday, Aug. 30   Pleasant and very warm. I did up my work in the morning, then Bert and I started for Canton as we both wanted to get some things. We went around by Little River to get the horses shod. I stopped at Mr. Wells while Dol was shod then we left Fred there and went to town. I took Mrs. Gillette's book home and did quite a bit of trading. It was so warm riding. Got a letter from Edith. In the evening I was all alone in the house until about 12 o'clock. Bert carried Mr. and Mrs. Crossman to Pierpont. Mr. Pitt said he saw Uncle Austin in Hanawa and he would soon be here.

Sunday, Aug. 31   Pleasant and very warm. I did up my work and got my mail ready to send in the morning. Wrote three letters and did up two rolls of papers. I read some, quite a bit in fact. Was kind of lonesome as usual. I sat out on the porch quite a while just at night. It was a little cooler then.

SEPTEMBER

Monday, Sept. 1   Cloudy and rainy most all day. The sun shone out a few times. It rained very hard in the afternoon. I did up my work and laid down a while. I did some mending after I got up. In the afternoon Marvie, Fannie and the baby came and staid all night. Just before dark I walked down to see if there was any mail but didn't find any.

Tuesday, Sept. 2   Pleasant and cooler. Marvie's folks didn't get started until between 10 & 11 o'clock. Then I did some work. That man that was here a year ago selling medicine and extracts was here today. (What he asked me.) In the afternoon I just fussed around. Felt awful tired. Walked down for the mail and got a letter from Mr. Stiles. I played on the organ a lot in the afternoon.

Wednesday, Sept. 3   Very pleasant. Mr. Pitt came down for some milk this morning, and he talked quite a long while with me. I did up my work and got all ready to go down town if I saw a chance to ride. I walked down to the corner and staid in to Mrs. Poole's about 2 hrs. waiting for a chance but got none so I came back home. I read quite a bit in the afternoon. Dear, it seems as if I would go crazy thinking about things. Walked down for the mail in the afternoon and got letters from Edith and Lena. Wrote to Edith.

Thursday, Sept. 4   Rained in the morning and was cloudy all the forenoon, but was very pleasant in the afternoon except a shower toward night. I went to the village in the forenoon and got back at 2:30. Had my picture taken at Runions' and did some trading. Got a letter from Charlie. Julia O'Brien who used to go to school when I did came in on the noon train and rode up with me. I carried her up to Mr. Howard's. We had a great visit, talked every minute.

Friday, Sept. 5   Very pleasant and nice and cool. I worked about all day canning crab apples and made jelly besides doing my common work. I walked down for the mail soon after it was time for it to come. Got my proofs of my pictures and a fine letter from Mr. R. and one from Aunt Susan. One of the proofs was very good but the other two weren't good. Wrote to Mr. R. in the evening. My jelly was late cooking down.

Saturday, Sept. 6 Pleasant. I walked down to the corner to send my mail by the stage in the morning and had to wait quite a while. Worked all day long until most night, sweeping, dusting, washing windows, cleaning the plant shelf, bringing water etc. Was awful tired. Just at night I walked down for the mail and got the "Universalist Leader" and a St. Louis paper and two pictures with it. I read a little in the evening then went to bed.

Sunday, Sept. 7 Pleasant. It rained in the night last night. I had a little work left over for this morning, arranging the table, picking a bouquet, cleaning the lamps etc. Then I made some Tapioca pudding. Then I took a bath and changed my clothes and read. In the afternoon Mrs. Stiles called on me and took me for a ride. I read some in the evening. Talked with Mr. Pitt a few minutes in the morning when he came down for the milk. Uncle Nelson and Aunt Louise were going by and drove in to see me.

Monday, Sept. 8 Very pleasant. After I got my work done up in the morning I spent all the forenoon reading a book for girls. In the afternoon I looked over some of my old keepsakes and fussed around. Walked down for the mail and got a letter from Edith. I wrote to Edith and Lena. Read some in the evening.

Tuesday, Sept. 9 Very windy but aside from that it was pleasant until about 4 o'clock when it began to rain and rained quite hard. I walked down to the corner to send my letters by the stage in the morning and was in to Mrs. Poole's a little while. Mr. Blackman came up to help Bert get in a little grain and Bert asked me to get dinner for them so I did. Had green corn for dinner. It tasted good. In the afternoon I walked down for the mail and the wind most blew me away. Got a letter from Charlie. Laid down a few minutes and read a little. Wrote to Charlie as he wanted me to answer his letter right off.

Wednesday, Sept. 10 Very pleasant. I worked up stairs all day long and was very tired. I swept and dusted the three rooms, took out all the windows and washed them and moved everything back and forth. Just at night I walked down for the mail and got a letter from Edith. Wrote to her in the evening. My rooms look very nice tonight, if I am so tired. It was real cool.

Thursday, Sept. 11   Very pleasant. I woke up between 4 & 5 o'clock sick. Got up at 5 and built a fire and got something hot and then went back to bed, then got up again about 8 and got my breakfast and did up my work, then I changed my clothes and got ready to go to town. I played on the organ a little and read a little. In the afternoon Mrs. Carter came down and staid to supper and until most 7 o'clock. We had a good visit. I walked along with her down for the mail. Got letters from Mr. R. and Bertha Lewis, and got a paper and picture from Mr. R. His letter was all right. Read the article that Edith wrote for the "Plaindealer."

Friday, Sept. 12   Very pleasant. I got up kind of early and got my breakfast and got ready to go down town. Started about 7 o'clock and drove up to Uncle Nelson's first to get the papers to send to Mert and Irma and I also wanted to see Mr. Endersbee. Then I drove to Canton. Got one of my pictures and sent it to Edith. They are real good. I did some trading and staid in town until about 10:30 then started for home getting home at noon. I laid down in the afternoon about 2 hrs. Then went for the mail and sewed some.

Saturday, Sept. 13   Cloudy and rainy until about 3 o'clock in the afternoon, when the sun shone out at intervals. It didn't rain hard at all but we had little showers. I did my Saturday's work and got through a little after noon then I changed my clothes and walked down for the mail. Got letters from Edith and Mr. R. and both of the letters made me feel kind of bad. I wrote to them right off. We had a lovely sunset and it was a pleasant moonlight night. (Edith's birthday.)

Sunday, Sept. 14   Very pleasant. I read and thought most all day, played on the organ a little and wrote a little more to both Edith and Mr. R. Went for a walk up in the pasture just at night. It was fine out. I was lonesome and blue today. Went to bed early. Had roast corn for dinner.

Monday, Sept. 15   Pleasant, very pleasant. I got up early and did up my work and went down town. Got back about 1 o'clock, took care of my horse, ate some lunch, and took care of my clothes then walked down for the mail. Just before I got to the corner saw Charlie coming. Lula and the baby were with him. I was so glad to see him. We talked and he ate supper with me and as usual we didn't go to bed until quite late or "early". Got his letter.

Tuesday, Sept. 16   Pleasant. Charlie ate breakfast and supper with me and dinner out there. The threshers came today but didn't fasten up any. They tried to get Charlie to help thresh but he wouldn't. We visited all day long and I was so glad to have him here. Just at night we walked down for the mail but there wasn't any, then we walked up the road to the top of the hill and sat on a rock for quite a while.

Wednesday, Sept. 17   Pleasant. I did up my work, took a bath, and got ready for the fair before dinner besides spending some time talking to Charlie. In the afternoon we went to the fair. Had a good time. Saw Jim McMinn up on the seat, and when we went off from the Grandstand he gave the little whistle call that he used to give when he was going with me and would be going home at night. We got here about dark. Charlie bought a basket of pears, and we ate part of them coming home. The fair is fine this year. Got a letter from Edith.

Thursday, Sept. 18   Pleasant. Bert and Lula went to the fair in the afternoon and had the little Robinson girl up here to take care of the baby. Charlie and I staid at home and talked and did what work we had to. In the afternoon Lena and Mr. Hastings came up and staid quite a while. We had a good time. Mert and Irma called just at night or in the evening, on their way back from the fair. Charlie and I went down for the mail in the evening and sat on the side of the road in the moonlight for a while. I got a paper and two pictures from Mr. R.

Friday, Sept. 19   Pleasant. I did up the work and talked with Charlie a while then we got ready and drove down town and I mailed some handkerchiefs for Kathleen's birthday. Went up to see if my pictures were done but they weren't. We drove up to see Lena and she took a ride with us around town. She wanted us to stay in the afternoon and go up the river with her and Mr. Hastings on a picnic but Charlie didn't want to go. Toward night we started to go for a ride and Bert wanted us to get some medicine for the baby so we went down town again. I wrote a postal to Mert.

Saturday, Sept. 20   Pleasant until toward night, when it rained hard. I pretended to do my Saturday's work but could hardly spend time for it for Charlie and I wanted to just sit and talk. He walked down for the mail in the afternoon while I was doing some work but didn't find any mail. He ate supper with Bert's folks but most of the time he has eaten with me.

Sunday, Sept. 21   Very pleasant. I got up about 7 o'clock I think and got breakfast, then Charlie and I got ready to go to Norwood. We started about 9 o'clock and got to Mert's to dinner. They had a nice dinner and we had a good time. In the afternoon Charlie and I, Mert and Irma and baby Maud all went over to Will's and staid for supper. Aunt Mercy came there a few minutes to see us. After supper we all went back to Mert's and went down and looked his shop over then Charlie and I started for home. Had a lovely drive both ways. We have such fine days and moonlight nights.

Monday, Sept. 22   Pleasant. I did up the work with Charlie's help, and then we talked until dinner time. Then I got dinner and we did up the work again. Toward night we got ready and drove up to the wood lot and looked that over. I asked Charlie if he would go up there with me. Then we drove down town and I got my pictures. Had another fine drive. I got letters from Edith, Mr. R. and Mr. Stiles. We stopped at Uncle Nelson's on our way back from the wood lot and talked a few minutes. (Mama's birthday.)

Tuesday, Sept. 23   Pleasant. I partly did up the work then spent my time with Charlie as he was going home. How I hated to have him go. He is so good to me, I enjoy having him here. He didn't start for home until after 3 o'clock. I cried when he went. I came up stairs and laid down and went to sleep. Walked down for the mail in the afternoon. Oh, I am lonesome and worried again. If I could only understand myself and be sure what I want to do.

Wednesday, Sept. 24   Pleasant, but real cool. I worked about all day sweeping, dusting and slicking up. Oh, I am so lonesome, and so nervous and worried. I walked down for the mail in the afternoon but only got the "Plaindealer." I wrote to Edith and Mr. Roberts. Oh, if I only knew what to do.

Thursday, Sept. 25   Pleasant and cool. I did quite a bit of work. These are awful days for me. I don't know what to do and am so lonesome and discouraged and nervous. In the afternoon I walked down for the mail and got letters from Edith and Charlie. I cried over his letter. Got a St. Louis paper and the "Universalist Leader" too. I wrote to Charlie toward night. Read some in the evening and went to bed early.

Friday, Sept. 26   Rainy, just a kind of a mist. I did up my work and washed out a few clothes etc. Bert's folks went to the village. He brought the mail when he came back. I got letters from Edith and Larnard and a big box of beautiful flowers from Edith for Papa's and Mama's graves and my "Ladies' Home Journal." Oh, I have been so lonesome again today. I feel like crying all the time. I got quite a lot of mail ready to send tomorrow.

Saturday, Sept. 27   Pleasant and very warm. It sprinkled a little in the afternoon. I did up my work and got ready to go down town. Started about 10 o'clock. Took the flowers that Edith sent along to the cemetary. Went up to Mr. Jackson's with him to dinner and had a good visit. Spent most of the afternoon with Kittie up on the balcony at Miss Heffernan's store, watching an auction. Saw Zuar when I was ready to start for home and talked with him quite a while. Got a postal from Edith.

Sunday, Sept. 28   Tried to rain but didn't make out much. I did up my work, did some writing, laid down a while, then changed my clothes and read. I was lonesome, very lonesome. Toward night I walked up to Mr. Boyden's and called quite a little while then called at Mr. Pitt's a few minutes. I picked up some sweet apples under that tree by Mr. Pitt's.

Monday, Sept. 29   Kind of rainy in the morning but came off pleasant and warm. I did up my work, then did some work up stairs, copied some receipts, looked over some papers etc. I was awful lonesome. In the afternoon I brought water to wash with tomorrow. Laid down a while. Walked down for the mail toward night. Just at night Uncle Ing came but he staid in the other part of the house, came in to see me a few minutes. I suppose Charlie started tonight. It makes me feel so lonesome just to think of it.

Tuesday, Sept. 30   Pleasant mostly, sprinkled a little a few times. Uncle Ing ate breakfast with me and visited quite a while, then he drove Dol down town and back at night. He talked with me quite a while again at night. I did an awful big washing and it was hard work for of course, I had to bring all the water myself. I worked up to about 4 o'clock. Eva Hosley called on me and brought a note from her Mama. I walked along to the corner with her after the mail when she went. She stayed quite a while.

OCTOBER

Wednesday, Oct. 1   Kind of rainy in the morning then staid pleasant until about 3 o'clock when it began to rain and rained hard. Uncle Ing ate breakfast with me then went to town for the day to Court. He got back about 4 o'clock and ate supper with me then he went up to Uncle Nelson's. I walked along to the corner with him to get the mail. Got a letter from Edith. I washed out my colored clothes, emptied all the water, swept, mopped, and cleaned the steps and porch etc. Then I took a bath and changed my clothes.

Thursday, Oct. 2   Cloudy until late in the afternoon when the sun shone out. I did my work and then changed my clothes and read what leisure time I had because it was my birthday. Uncle Nelson and Uncle Ing called this morning and left my umbrella and a package that Mrs. Carter sent down. It was a book for me to read and a little booklet that she sent me wishing me many returns of the day. It was kind of her. I walked down for the mail in the afternoon and got a fine letter from Mr. Roberts. Wrote to Mr. R. in the evening.

Friday, Oct. 3   Pleasant. I did up my work, set out some plants that I had rooting and did a few little odd jobs then ironed. About 2 o'clock I changed my clothes and about 3 went down for the mail. I found a box full, a letter from Charlie, a package from Mr. Roberts which was two very nice books for my birthday, a package from Edith which was a picture and two papers and the St. Louis paper with two pictures with it, so I had a great treat. I wrote to Edith and Mr. R. in the evening, thanking them for the presents.

Saturday, Oct. 4   Pleasant and cool. In the morning I walked down to the corner to send some mail and called at Mrs. Poole's. We had a frost last night. I ironed, baked bread, beans, cake, swept, dusted, and mopped and in fact put in a big day's work and was tired. Toward night I changed my clothes and walked down for the mail. Got a good letter from Edith. I finished reading the book, "First Love Is Best,"[12] in the evening. Bert's folks went to town in the evening and Curly and I were alone until about 11 o'clock. Sent my butter jar.

Sunday, Oct. 5   Cool and cloudy. I did up my work then took a bath and changed my clothes, and read until about 3 o'clock in the afternoon when I was taken sick and was so awful sick and all alone too.

It was dreadful. I tried to lie down but part of the time couldn't stay there at all but had to get up again. Oh, I was in such pain. I was that way until 8 o'clock in the evening when I quieted down and undressed and went to bed.

Monday, Oct. 6   Cloudy and rainy and pleasant by turns. Uncle Ing came down here from Uncle Nelson's before I had my breakfast. I hadn't had anything to eat for about 20 hours. I got all ready to go to town, Uncle Ing and I, to get some things but Bert said he was going to town and was going to use the horses so Uncle Ing went with him and got some things then he fixed the cellar wall for me. He was here to dinner and supper. I brought in wood and water and it was hard work as I didn't feel well at all. Walked down for the mail and got a letter from Charlie. Rode part way back with Mr. Scott. Wrote to Charlie in the evening.

Tuesday, Oct. 7   Pleasant in the morning but clouded up and rained in the afternoon. I did up my work, mended my waists and whatever clothes I had that were to be starched. I mended them and starched them and fixed my hat. I laid down in the afternoon but the flies bothered me and I got nervous so I didn't go to sleep but rested. I sent two letters this morning. Wrote one of them this morning and part of the other one. In the evening I played on the organ for about an hour and a half for I was so sad and lonesome.

Wednesday, Oct. 8   Real cold all day, very cold in the morning. Pleasant. I did up my work and then mended. Had a great time finding my winter underclothes that I put away this spring. I walked down for the mail in the afternoon but found an empty box. I was disappointed. I read some in the evening and wrote some more to Edith. Finished the letter I partly wrote last night. I am so lonesome.

Thursday, Oct. 9   Cloudy and cold in the morning but it came off pleasant after a while. I ironed my five waists and that finished up my ironing. I did up my work, also ironed two neck ribbons and pressed my black skirt. In the afternoon I walked down for the mail and got letters from Edith, Mr. R. and Mabel Lewis and some papers. Edith's letter asked me to meet them at the train Saturday night. Oh, I am so glad. I walked back down to Mr. Poole's to see if I could get him to bring up her trunk and up to Mr. Pitt's to see if he knew where I could get some wood.

Friday, Oct. 10   Very pleasant. I worked hard until 1 o'clock then Mrs. Carter came down and wanted me to go to the woods with her so we went up to the spring. She had quite a talk with me. I walked down for the mail after we got back (after 4 o'clock) and then walked up to Mr. Pitt's to see about the wood. I picked up a sack full of sweet apples and brought them home. This forenoon I put outing blankets on all the beds and got things ready for Edith, swept and dusted up stairs and down only I didn't get it all done before Mrs. C. came.

Saturday, Oct. 11   Warm and pleasant. I finished slicking up the house, dusting, mopping, washing windows, bringing water etc. besides the common work. After dinner I took a bath and changed my clothes and got ready to go down and meet Edith and the children. Started about 4 o'clock. Had good luck all around. We came down from the train in the "Bus" and had some pleasant company. Saw Zuar and talked with him a while. (In the meat shop.) We had a big load coming home, lots of groceries, satchels, wraps, Edith, the three children and I. I held Carroll and drove. We did not go to bed until 12 o'clock.

Sunday, Oct. 12   Kind of a mist and rained a little bit. We did the work and I just enjoyed the children the rest of the time. Uncle Ing came down and staid to dinner and Uncle Nelson and Aunt Louise came down in the afternoon and staid quite a while. I wasn't lonesome today. Wrote to Mert in the evening. I suppose Mr. R. says goodbye to St. Louis tomorrow morning.[13]

Monday, Oct. 13   Very windy, and pleasant part of the time and rainy part of the time. We did quite a washing but had to leave the clothes in the rinsing water because it was so windy. Did the common work too which was quite a bit to do. I was tired carrying so much water and working so. Just at night Carroll and I went down for the mail but there wasn't any. We rode back with Mr. Poole. We had a big time, Carroll and I today. The dear little fellow. The three children keep things lively.

Tuesday, Oct. 14   Pleasant and quite cool. We finished up the washing and did the other work. I was so tired for I carried so much water. I worked all day. Edith made some ginger cookies. Bert's folks went to the village and I sent for a few things by him. I popped a pan of corn for the children. Had fun with them today of course. We all took a bath in the evening before we went to bed. Mr. Pitt stopped in this morning to see the children and Edith.

Wednesday, Oct. 15   Cold and cloudy. In the afternoon it rained. Mrs. Hosley called in the forenoon. I worked most all day, played with the children some. I made a pie and Edith made bread. I walked down for the mail just at night. It was muddy and not very good walking. I didn't get any letters today either. How I wish I knew what I was going to do.

Thursday, Oct. 16   Pleasant. I worked all day or about all day. It was Carroll's birthday, and I gave him a necktie and made a birthday cake for him. Mr. C. sent a box of presents and among them was a long neck ribbon for me. Carroll and I went down for the mail in the afternoon. I got a letter from Mr. R. He didn't leave St. Louis until Tuesday night. I looked for him all day today until I got that letter. I dusted all over besides doing all the other work. Oh, if I only knew what to do. It is enough to kill anybody to be as I am just now.[14]

Friday, Oct. 17   Very pleasant. I didn't have as much to do today. Just the common work and waiting on the children some. Fred Billings called in the morning to see about buying cows. Edith walked up to Mrs. Pitt's in the forenoon and the children stayed with me. In the afternoon Carroll and I went for the mail. I got a letter from Irma in answer to the one I wrote to Mert. Then we staid outdoors a while and saw the pigs and played with the dog etc. that dear little man and I. I kind of looked for Mr. R. today and yet didn't hardly expect him.

Saturday, Oct. 18   Pleasant in the morning but began to rain in the afternoon and rained hard just at night and in the evening. I worked until about 3 o'clock. Made a batch of doughnuts. Walked down for the mail about 3 o'clock, then came home and took a bath and changed my clothes. Bert was away and didn't get home until late. Oh, I am so discouraged tonight over everything, I don't know what to do. I can't stand such works much longer.

Sunday, Oct. 19   Pleasant most all day but we had a shower in the forenoon and in the evening it rained hard and thundered and lightened. Mert, Irma, and baby Maud came out, got here in the forenoon or before dinner, and staid until after supper. The children all had a big time and we enjoyed watching them. I thought Mr. Roberts would be here today but he hasn't come yet. It is too bad. Mr. and Mrs. Boyden called just at night.

Monday, Oct. 20   Pleasant most all day but it rained some toward night. Edith did a big washing and I helped some and did a lot of other work. I felt very bad all day. I changed my clothes just at night and went down for the mail. Got a letter from Mr. R. saying perhaps he would come in on the evening train so I hurried around and drove to Canton but he didn't come. I saw Lena and talked with her quite a while. Came home by moonlight and took care of my own horse.

Tuesday, Oct. 21   Pleasant. Such a time as I had in the forenoon. Bert didn't do the milking and I didn't know it until between 8 & 9 o'clock then I walked up to Mr. Pitt's first, then down to Mr. Robinson's, then to Herbie Bullis' to get someone to milk. Mr. Bullis and Herbie came and milked. Then I hitched up and drove to Canton and stopped along the road to see if I could get a man. When I drove into town I saw Mr. R. first. He went around with me to get the things then we came home. He did the milking and chores at night. We staid up all night talking.

Wednesday, Oct. 22   Kind of pleasant, until toward night when it began to rain. Everything was in an uproar today for Bert's folks were moving.[15] They got started "bag and baggage" about 2 o'clock. I asked Bert to come in here and talk things over. After they had gone Mr. R. and I went over to the barns and looked things over. We all did quite a bit of work. We went to bed between 11 & 12. Mr. R. got the mail out of the box this morning and I got a fine but sad letter from Charlie. It made me cry. Oh, if I only knew what to do. It nearly makes me crazy.

Thursday, Oct. 23   Pleasant and cold. I spent kind of a queer day of it. Went over to the barn in the morning and talked with Mr. R. quite a while and in the afternoon I went over to the horse barn and staid quite a while. No, that was in the forenoon. We were late getting up and late with our work. Just at night I walked down for the mail. Went to bed between 12 and 1. Sewed the buttons on his overcoat in the evening.

Friday, Oct. 24   Kind of dull and cloudy. I just fussed around and worked around as usual. Oh, dear such times. How I wish things were different and that I knew what to do. I am so tired of everything.

Saturday, Oct. 25   Pleasant and cold. I did a little work in the morning. Then Mr. R. and I drove to Potsdam. I stopped at Uncle Ing's, had dinner there and staid until he came back. We didn't get home until about dark, then I drove down for the mail. Had a pretty good time.

Sunday, Oct. 26   Cloudy part of the time and pleasant part of the time. I had some extra work to do today because I was gone yesterday. John Kennedy and Eva called when we were eating dinner. Mrs. Pitt came down and staid quite a while. Mr. Stiles called in the afternoon. It was night again before we knew it.

Monday, Oct. 27　　　Quite pleasant, kind of windy. I did a big day's work and was tired, and feel so sad and blue. Edith went down for the mail toward night and found some apples in the road that a man lost off from a load of apples. She and Carroll went back and picked up some of them then Carroll and I went and picked up the rest.

Tuesday, Oct. 28　　　Quite pleasant. I did all sorts of things as I do now every day. Such a hard time as it is for me. Mr. R. and I didn't go to bed until 3 o'clock but staid up talking. Such a talk as we had. I did what ironing I had to do and what common work there was to do.

Wednesday, Oct. 29　　　Quite pleasant but cold. It was the same old story today. I am just kind of existing now. Josie Boyden, she that was, came down in the afternoon and staid quite a while. Ella came for her and called, too. Mr. Pitt left me between 2 & 3 bushels of apples. Mr. R. said something that hurt my feelings today. Oh, how sick and tired I am of everything.

Thursday, Oct. 30　　　All kinds of weather—spring, summer, autumn, and winter. We did the work and after dinner Edith, the children, and I went down to the cemetary. It rained coming back and was cold. Such a time as I had when I got back. I cried from then until after dark and staid in the parlor in the cold. Oh, how much longer have I got to feel like this. It is terrible. I began to feel sick at night.

Friday, Oct. 31　　　Pleasant. I worked all the forenoon and in the afternoon. Mr. Roberts, Carroll, and I went to Canton. We got back just at dark. I had a talk with Edith in the evening. How I wish I knew what to do. I don't go to bed any night until between 12 & 1 on such a matter.

NOVEMBER

Saturday, Nov. 1　　　Very pleasant. We were doing up our work when Aunt Mercy, Hat, Pauline, Net, and Ethel drove in. We had a great day out of it. We had a big table full for dinner and supper. Aunt Mercy, Hat, and Pauline staid all night. Such a time as they all had over my position just now.[16] Just before dark I walked down to the factory after my jar of butter. Aunt Mercy slept with me. We had a big day's work to do too but didn't do it all. They all fell in love with Mr. R.

Sunday, Nov. 2   Very pleasant and warm. I did quite a bit of work in the forenoon even if it was Sunday. They started for home about 10 o'clock. When dinner was ready today, I went up in the lot to meet Mr. R. and Carroll. They had been to the woods. In the afternoon Mr. R., Carroll and I drove up to the wood lot. Had a pretty good time. He got a lot of pretty ferns.

Monday, Nov. 3   Quite pleasant. We had a big washing. Edith did most of that, but I was busy all day too doing other work. Was so tired and discouraged. Mr. R. painted the tin roof. He went after the mail today. I felt very lonesome and sad today.

Tuesday, Nov. 4   Very pleasant, just like summer. We worked until in the afternoon then Edith, the children and I went for a ride around the square and called at Mr. Boyden's and talked with the folk at Rodee's. We had Fred horse and he felt good and Edith was frightened.

Wednesday, Nov. 5   Very pleasant and warm. We worked all day. Mr. R. and Carroll went after a load of wood up to Mr. Allen's. In the afternoon Gertie Wallace came down. Aunt Louise and Mrs. Carter called a few minutes. We didn't go to bed until 2 o'clock, Mr. R. and I.

Thursday, Nov. 6   Kind of a queer day, rained part of the time and the wind blew then it was pleasant part of the time. I did what work I had to do and spent part of my time bothering Mr. Roberts. I took a bath in the afternoon and changed my clothes then went down for the mail but found an empty box. I went to bed early, about 8 o'clock.

Friday, Nov. 7   Quite pleasant, kind of cool. I hurried with the work this morning then carried Edith and the children up to Uncle Nelson's. I came back and Mr. R. took the rig and went to Potsdam. Then I changed my clothes and walked back up there. We staid until after supper then Uncle Nelson and Mr. Carter hitched up to bring us all home. Just as we got started we met Mr. R. so Carroll and I rode with him and Mr. C. went back.

Saturday, Nov. 8   Very pleasant. I hurried and did what work I had to do then got ready to go to Canton. Mr. R. and I started about 10:30. I had a lot of trading to do. Such times as I had hearing what people said and such times trying to get a dressmaker to do some work for me.[17] Saw

Bert in Canton and he came up here just ahead of us and staid all night. I did quite a bit of work after I got home and did quite an ironing in the evening.

Sunday, Nov. 9   A beautiful day. I had a lot of work to do in the forenoon. Had to settle up business with Bert. He left here just a little while before dinner. Dolph, Net, and Ethel were here to dinner and then went to Mrs. Mead's funeral. Edith and I went and took baby. Carroll and Kathleen staid with Mr. Roberts. When we were coming home we met Mr. and Mrs. Gardner and Earl. Maud Boyden Hill called here while we were gone to the funeral.

Monday, Nov. 10   Quite pleasant. We did a big day's work. Had a good sized washing to do and lots of other work. Mr. R. and Carroll worked in the front yard, cleaning it up. Got a postal from Kittie. I made a maple sugar frosted cake without any egg and it was fine. Kathleen said "Aunt Mabel" for the first time today and thought it was awful cute. Carroll wanted me to do everything for him today.

Tuesday, Nov. 11   Pleasant. I did another big day's work. Worked all day long. Made some cookies today without eggs and they were real good too. Wrote two short letters this morning. Mr. R. and Carroll finished cleaning up the yard and it looks much better. He, Mr. R., had a bonfire out of the leaves.

Wednesday, Nov. 12   Cloudy and rainy. I went out to the barn in the forenoon and staid until dinner time. Had a great talk with Mr. R. and had a big cry. Did quite a bit of work in the afternoon. Took a bath in the afternoon and walked down for the mail just at night but there wasn't any. Oh, such times as I have with myself. I will be so glad if I ever get settled down in some way. It grew colder toward night and was very cold.

Thursday, Nov. 13   It stormed all night last night, and this morning everything was covered with ice. I did quite a lot of work, worked about all day. I thought of going down town today but gave it up until tomorrow. It was quite pleasant today. Went down for the mail in the afternoon and got a postal from Mrs. Griffith. I made a lovely cake for supper without any eggs.

Friday, Nov. 14   Kind of rainy in the morning but came off pleasant then rained some in the afternoon too. I did what work I had to do in the morning, then Mr. R. and I went down town. Such a time as I put in, I had so much to do. Got a letter from George Johnston, a good one. I also got a fine picture of Charlie Nichols all framed. I didn't stop to eat anything until supper time after breakfast. Mr. R. and I staid up until about 2 o'clock. We had a great talk.

Saturday, Nov. 15   Warm and pleasant. I did what work I could. Right after dinner Edith and I went to Grandma Barnes funeral. Will, Hat, Aunt Mercy, Eva and Pauline came here to dinner and went to the funeral. Mr. R. took care of the three children for us. We put in quite a day of it. I went to bed quite early. Had a great time trying to get some snarls out of my hair in the evening, or Edith did rather.

Sunday, Nov. 16   Quite pleasant, only it was cloudy. I had quite a bit of work to do today that I couldn't get done yesterday. Uncle Nelson and Aunt Louise came down and staid about all day. All of the children wanted me to take them today.

Monday, Nov. 17   Quite pleasant. We did a big washing. Edith did most of it for it was mostly her clothes, and I did the other work. Worked all day. I went to bed at 8 o'clock. I was very tired. Mr. R. went up to the Mills and got quite a bit of work done at the shop.

Tuesday, Nov. 18   Rained some in the morning but was quite pleasant the rest of the time. I did what common work there was today. In the afternoon Mr. and Mrs. Cole and their little girl came and staid until after supper. We had a good visit. I had to hurry around and get things ready for supper. Went to bed in good season.

Wednesday, Nov. 19   Very pleasant. I did up the work, or part of it, wrote three letters and got one of my pictures done up ready to send away, walked down to the factory (Mrs. Poole's) to borrow a little butter and got dinner in the forenoon. Then I took a bath and got ready to go down town. Mr. R. and I went. I tried on my dress at Mrs. Griffith's and had quite a talk with her. I did a little trading too. We came home after dark most of the way.

Thursday, Nov. 20   Very pleasant. I hurried around and did up the work in the morning and about 11 o'clock we all, Mr. R., Edith, Carroll, Kathleen, Helene and I started for Canton. We ate dinner at Dr. Russell's and went around calling in the afternoon, made 8 or 9 calls. Started for home about 5 o'clock. Had a pleasant time but we were tired. I got an announcement of Dora Taylor's marriage and a letter from Aunt Laurinda.

Friday, Nov. 21   Quite pleasant but kind of cloudy. I did a big day's work. Washed what dirty clothes there were besides doing quite a bit of other work. A little while before dinner, Mrs. Carter came down and staid until about 4 o'clock. Just at supper time Mr. R. and I had such a time. I went to bed early.

Saturday, Nov. 22   It rained most all day. Such a day of it as I had. I cried most all day, I felt so badly. Oh, such times, if the thing is ever all settled, how glad I'll be. It was warm and pleasant in the morning but soon clouded up and began to rain. I did quite a bit of work in the afternoon and ironed in the evening, and patched Mr. R.'s clothes. Got a letter from George Johnston.

Sunday, Nov. 23   Pleasant and cold. All frozen up. I had another hard time this morning. How it all worries me. Mr. Pitt came down just before we had our dinner and staid a while. He brought two cabbages and two turnips. In the afternoon Mr. R. made popcorn balls. They were fine. Baby didn't sleep in the evening and I took her in the parlor with us, the dear little thing.

Monday, Nov. 24   Pleasant part of the time and rainy part of the time. We didn't wash and I didn't go to town. I did quite a bit of work. Walked down for the mail in the afternoon and got a letter from Mrs. Griffith. I was sick at night, began about supper time and had to go to bed right after supper and leave the dishes. Had quite a time getting to sleep.

Tuesday, Nov. 25   Quite pleasant. I felt poorly all day but worked all day. Edith washed and I did the other work. Made doughnuts. Had a spell just after supper of being awful sick but felt better after a little. In the evening Mr. R. and I had an awful talk. Such times. It makes me most crazy.

Wednesday, Nov. 26   Very cold and snowed all day. I worked all the forenoon, then in the afternoon Mr. R. and I went to Canton. It was a cold stormy ride. I tried on my dress. It is lovely.

Thursday, Nov. 27   Pleasant and cold. I had another spell of feeling very badly. Just before dinner I had a big crying spell. Mr. R. tried to comfort me and so did dear little Carroll. We had chicken for dinner and had a pretty good dinner besides. Didn't go to bed very early. Tonight I promised Mr. R. for good that I would marry him, so it is settled.[18] God grant that I have done the right thing.

Friday, Nov. 28   Pleasant and cold. I did all sorts of odd jobs. I helped Mr. R. get the bobsleds down stairs in the horse barn. Edith was packing the box of things that she is going to take home, and Mr. R. helped her quite a bit. Edie and Fred called here. I wrote a letter to Mert and sent it by him. I went to bed in pretty good season.

Saturday, Nov. 29   Pleasant and warmer. I worked the most of the forenoon then Mr. R. and I got ready to go down town and started right after dinner. I got my dress. Got a fine letter from George Johnston.

Sunday, Nov. 30   Pleasant, and I am to be married today. How strange it seems. I did quite a lot of work, worked until about 2 o'clock, then went to get dressed. Mert came and I was so glad, so I had Edith and Mert and the children here just as I wanted them. Fred had to go to Potsdam to get his graduating suit. We had oysters for supper besides the other things. Mert staid all night too so we were all here. We stood between Papa and Mama's pictures to be married. It was a hard day for me. Dolph and Net called and so did Cora Pitt for a little while. Of course they didn't know there was anything out of the ordinary going on.[19]

DECEMBER

Monday, Dec. 1   Very pleasant. Mert started from home in the morning after he and Carroll had driven up to Uncle Nelson's. He took some things back with him. Right after dinner we all started for Canton. Dolph carried Edith, the children, and I down and Mr. R. took the trunk. We staid at Mrs. Wallace's overnight. Carroll and I went down street just before supper. The dear little man wouldn't get an inch away from me and slept with me. How will I ever get along without my precious little boy? Mrs. Pike called over to Mrs. Wallace's to see us. Mr. Drury called here in the morning and left us a pitcher of cider.

Tuesday, Dec. 2   We got up early to get ready to go to the depot. I dressed the dear little boy. How he clung to me, and when the train came in he cried as if his little heart would break. Oh, how I hated to have them go. It was so hard. There are so many hard things in my life. Mr. R. came down to go to the train and then we came home. I cried as hard as I could cry for a long time. We saw Aunt Mercy at Jessie Rodee's. She was glad to see us and we to see her. In the evening I directed 82 of the announcements, and now I enter into a new life. God grant that it may be the right kind of a life and a happy one.

Wednesday, Dec. 3   Rained most all day. I did quite a bit of work but felt poorly all day, that is, tired and sad. In the afternoon Mr. R. (I can't get used to calling him anything else) went to town and took the announcements. I made bean soup for supper and it tasted so good this damp rainy night. I played on the organ some in the afternoon while I was here alone. I went to bed early, was all in bed and most asleep when he came in from milking.

Thursday, Dec. 4   Pleasant and cold. I did my common work. Mr. R. fixed a horse blanket here in the forenoon and I helped (?) him. A squaw came along selling baskets. In the afternoon he went after a load of wood. I went for the mail, but there wasn't any. After supper I made a pie and some apple sauce and baked bread.

Friday, Dec. 5   Very cold. I just did my common work. Fred went to the village with the cattle and got Mr. Robinson to help him. He walked down after the mail toward night and got the rest of the announcements. We were late getting them for the stage driver didn't know where to leave them. I directed them in the evening and 6 papers besides ready to send away.

Saturday, Dec. 6   Still very cold. I did up part of my work, then we got ready to go down town. We started from here about 11 o'clock and got back about 3. I had lots of congratulations. How queer it seems. I went up to Mrs. Griffith's to see about my waist and in to Mrs. Kilbourn's to see about my hat and up to Mr. Whitmarsh's to get James Thompson's address from Aunt Laurinda. I got nice letters from Edith and Mabel Lewis.

Sunday, Dec. 7   Some warmer but snowed all day. I did my common work and spent considerable time talking to (my husband) and so the day was spent. We started an account book dating from the 1st of Dec. Wrote to Edith in the evening and to Carroll and Mr. R. wrote to Kathleen.

Monday, Dec. 8   Very cold. I just did my common work and a few little things besides. Spent quite a good deal of my time entertaining my husband. (That sounds queer.) He banked up the windows and around the places that needed it toward night. No mail today.

Tuesday, Dec. 9   Very cold. I just did my common work and then enjoyed myself the rest of the time. Fred dressed a chicken and did part of the sweeping for me. I made some bean soup for supper. In the evening we looked over my box of programs from Commencement and theatres. Didn't go to bed tonight until about 10 o'clock.

Wednesday, Dec. 10   Still very cold in the morning, but grew warmer all day and rained toward night. I just did the common work and "carried on" the rest of the time. Cooked the chicken for dinner. Found two of our big ducks killed today. Fred went after the mail. I got a letter from Edith and he one from Mrs. Abell. We also got a very pretty sugar spoon, silver with gold work, from Ella Boyden through the mail. The "Plaindealer" came too and I got another book from the Curio Company. Wrote to Edith in the evening.

Thursday, Dec. 11   Pleasant, a very fine day. I did up my work and we were going to the village but Uncle Nelson and Aunt Louise came. She was here to dinner and supper. He came back to supper and they staid a while in the evening. We had a good visit. I got a pretty good dinner and supper. They liked everything. I hemmed one of my new towels besides doing the house work. Fred went after the mail and we got letters from his brother Richard and from Mr. and Mrs. J. Blackman.

Friday, Dec. 12   Very pleasant and the sun shone, but it was cold. I did my common work and we talked quite a bit. In the afternoon we went down town and had a sleigh ride. I tried on my waist at Mrs. Griffith's and got my new hat. It is very pretty. We got letters from Mr. R.'s brother Allan and from the Chapmans and from Dr. Russell at Massena. It was a beautiful moonlight night when we came home.

Saturday, Dec. 13   Very cold, a bitter cold day. It was hard work to keep warm at all. We spent quite a lot of time talking for that was about all we could do. We ate dinner and supper on the little work table right in front of the fire. It was so cozy and cute. Mr. R. went after the mail and we got letters from Edith, Carroll, and Kathleen. I baked bread and beans.

Sunday, Dec. 14   Not as cold and very pleasant. We did up the work and slicked things all up. Had breakfast and dinner late because we were late getting up. Mathew Wallace stopped and gave us an invitation to a Grange Dance up to the Mills, a week from Friday night.

Monday, Dec. 15   Not as cold and real pleasant. We were late getting up this morning so it was nearly noon before I got ready to go to washing, and such a washing as I had. Haven't washed since Edith went home. Had to leave the colored clothes until tomorrow. Oh, but I was tired. Had about 14 sheets, spreads and tablecloths and everything else according. Fred helped me wash and got dinner and washed all the dishes. He went down for the mail and we got the two handsome presents from Edith's folks, the ½ doz. dessert spoons and the sofa pillow cover. I went to bed early. Didn't feel very good.

Tuesday, Dec. 16   It was much warmer and rained more or less all day, and the wind blew. We had to bring in all the clothes, rinse and wring them again, and put up more lines in the house for them to hang on, and wash the colored clothes. Such a washing. I was so tired I cried and laughed both. No mail today. I went up stairs and laid down a while on my own bed in the afternoon and went to sleep. It seemed good.

Wednesday, Dec. 17   Pleasant. I did the common work, did some work up stairs and made some ginger cookies etc. I felt kind of bad in the morning, that is, felt blue but got over it about noon. In the afternoon I didn't do much of anything but sit in my husband's lap. He went after the mail just at dusk. I got a letter from Edith that made me feel badly or something she said did. I had quite a crying spell. It snowed some today.

Thursday, Dec. 18   It was pleasant in the morning, then began to snow and snowed very hard, but finally stopped. We had a lunch dinner and started for town about noon. Such a time as I had buying Xmas presents. I hadn't bought a thing for Xmas until today. We didn't start for home until after dark. Saw Aunt Mercy in the window at Jessie Rodee's as we went by and waved my hand to her. Got a letter from Aunt Susan. Heard that Mert had a position as station agent in Raymondville.[20]

Friday, Dec. 19   Pleasant. In the forenoon I didn't work very hard, but in the afternoon I put in every minute. Swept and dusted the chambers and slicked them all up. Such a job but it looked fine when I got through. I was awful tired at night. Got a letter from Aunt Mercy. Mr. R. went to the Mills in the afternoon.

Saturday, Dec. 20   Pleasant, very much so part of the time for the sun shone out. In the forenoon I just kind of fussed around doing odd little jobs and in the afternoon I worked hard again. Wrote a line to Aunt Mercy and Mr. R. took it down and got the mail. Got a letter from Edith.

In the evening Cora and Milton Pitt came down and spent the evening. I had some work to do after they went home. Didn't get to bed until 11 o'clock. I was so tired again.

Sunday, Dec. 21   Quite pleasant in the morning, but it began to rain and freeze on and in the afternoon it was very bad. I did my work and started a letter to Aunt Susan when Aunt Mercy came in the afternoon. Fred made popcorn balls and started candy but didn't have very good luck with it and left it until morning. We had a good visit but went to bed in pretty good season.

Monday, Dec. 22   Dull and cloudy all day. Right after breakfast I began to feel sick and grew worse. Oh, I was awful sick, it seemed as if I couldn't stand it. Such a time. I wanted to do so much and couldn't do anything. Aunt Mercy did up the work and got dinner. Late in the afternoon I got up and Aunt Mercy and I made the bags for the popcorn and candy for Xmas. Fred got the mail and I got a letter from Lena and the package of presents from Edith's came. He finished up the candy and it was good. We had another good visit in the evening and I did quite a lot of writing also.

Tuesday, Dec. 23   Pleasant and cold. In the forenoon we spent all of our time nearly, getting the boxes of presents all ready to send and all the mail. Then I got some dinner and we started. We took the double buggy and carried Aunt Mercy over to Net's first then went to Canton. We didn't get home until quite late. Sent all of the packages and I went up and tried on my waist at Mrs. Griffith's.

Wednesday, Dec. 24   Quite pleasant. I didn't feel very well today and the work dragged. Mrs. Carter drove over late in the afternoon and asked us if we couldn't come up there in the evening but we were going to town. We drove to town in the evening and up to Uncle Nelson's first with their presents. I got my waist and we got several presents through the mail. Got a beautiful clock from Fred's brother Richard and his picture and Eva's picture and a silver butter knife from Aunt Mercy. We didn't get to bed until very late.

Thursday, Dec. 25   Very pleasant. We went up to Uncle Nelson's about noon and were there to dinner and supper and a little while in the evening. Irma and little Maud were there and Uncle Ing and Aunt Nellie. We had a pleasant time. They all gave us presents and pretty ones. When we were coming back we got the mail. Got our wedding book and I got a letter and handkerchief from Aunt Laurinda. I did a lot of work in the forenoon.

Friday, Dec. 26   The work dragged again but I did quite a bit at last and didn't go to bed until about 12 o'clock. I was so tired and sleepy. I got a very pretty handkerchief from Aunt Susan through the mail. We had a great time getting our corner shelf put up and the clock on it. I was awful tired and nervous before I got to bed. Got a letter from Mert.

Saturday, Dec. 27   Very pleasant. I did an awful big day's work. Fred went down to the 11:15 train to meet his brother Allan. He is very nice. I like him ever so much. He brought us another very pretty lamp and brought a sack of lovely grapes. I was so tired and worried over the work. Got a letter from Edith and a note and two handkerchiefs from Aunt Mercy, one for me and one for him. Didn't get to bed until late.

Sunday, Dec. 28   Very pleasant. I had quite a lot of work to do today but got it all done up about noon then took a bath and changed my clothes. Fred went up to the wood lot. We had oysters for dinner. Before we were through Irma and little Maud came. We had lots of fun with little Maud.

Monday, Dec. 29   Quite pleasant in the morning but it got bad in the afternoon, the wind blew hard and the snow drifted and it stormed some, too. Irma and Maud staid until most dark, then Fred started to carry them home but Mr. Carter drove in for them just as they were getting ready to start. Little Maud was kind of sick most all day. Irma and I thought of going down town in the afternoon but the weather wouldn't let us. I wrote to Edith in the morning and to Eva in the evening. We had popcorn in the evening. Allan washed the dishes for me tonight.

Tuesday, Dec. 30   Pleasant. I did up my work and got it about all done in the forenoon then after the work was done up after dinner I changed my clothes and did whatever I wanted to. Allan went over to call on Mabel Hosley in the afternoon and Fred was over to the barn so I amused myself for a while playing on the organ. My brother-in-law washed all the dishes for me today and amused me with his talk. Fred went after the mail and got Don Blackman's picture and a very pretty doily for me from Mrs. Blackman. Both of the boys "carried on" in the evening and kept me laughing.

Wednesday, Dec. 31   Pleasant but quite windy. We were late getting up. I just did up my common work with the help that I have been having lately. Right after dinner Fred carried Allan to Potsdam and got his things that were out there. I was alone in the afternoon and part of the evening and was so lonesome and blue. I walked down for the mail through the drifts and in the wind. Got a letter from Edith and we got one from his brother George and wife and a roll of papers from Edith. I wrote some in the evening.

MEMORANDA

One more year ended. How I hope that the new year will bring me happiness. God grant that I may have the strength to do right and make life as pleasant as I can for myself and the one who is to share it with me and for all the people I may come in contact with. From now on my life will be different, whether better or worse or just about on the same plan I cannot tell. I can only hope for the best, and now 1902 with all of your sad times and your good times, good bye.

ε❧ Epilogue ❧ɜ

Mabel and Fred Roberts continued to live on the Wait farm throughout their lives. They had one daughter, Gladys, born in 1908. In addition to doing the farm work, Fred taught school in the Brick Chapel district. They both attended Grange functions in Crary Mills, and Mabel was active in the Presbyterian Ladies' Aid Society at Brick Chapel. Gladys attended the Brick Chapel primary school and high school in Canton and graduated from St. Lawrence University in 1929. Fred died in 1933 and Mabel in 1936. They are buried in the Wait family plot in the Brick Chapel cemetery.

The Wait farmhouse burned to the ground in 1938.

ৡ Notes ৄ

Notes to Introduction

[1] Marvin Wait is listed as "dairy farmer" in this history. See L. H. Everts, and J. M. Holcomb, ed., *History of St. Lawrence County, New York with Illustrations and Biographical Sketches of Some of Its Prominent Men and Pioneers* (Philadelphia: L. H. Everts & Co., 1878).

[2] These figures are based on neighbors' recollections and on deeds recorded in the St. Lawrence County Clerk's office.

[3] See Eunice R. Stamm, *The History of Cheese Making in New York State* (Endicott, New York: The Lewis Group, Ltd., 1991) for a description of the factory system. According to Curtis Gates's *Our County and Its People: A Memorial Record of St. Lawrence County, New York* (Syracuse: D. Mason & Co., 1894), there were 11 cheese factories in the town of Canton by 1877.

[4] For a discussion of the division of labor in farm families in New York during this period, see Sally McMurry, *Transforming Rural Life: Dairying Families and Agricultural Change, 1820–1885* (Baltimore: Johns Hopkins University Press, 1995) and Nancy Grey Osterud, *Bonds of Community: The Lives of Farm Women in Nineteenth Century New York* (Ithaca: Cornell University Press, 1991).

[5] For a discussion of the New Woman see Frances B. Cogan, *All-American Girl: The Ideal of Real Womanhood in Mid-Nineteenth-Century America* (Athens: The University of Georgia Press, 1989). For the standard description of the American Victorian domestic ideal of womanhood, see Barbara Welter, *Dimity Convictions: The American Woman in the Nineteenth Century* (Athens: Ohio University Press, 1976).

[6] Welter, 5.

[7] A rich literature exists on women's autobiography and women's diaries. Some of the most pertinent to the comments made here include Suzanne L. Bunkers and Cynthia A. Huff, "Issues in Studying Women's Diaries: A Theoretical and Critical Approach," in *Inscribing the Daily: Critical Essays on Women's Diaries,* ed. Suzanne L. Bunkers and Cynthia A. Huff (Amherst: U of Massachusetts Press, 1996); Margo Culley, "Introduction," in *A Day at a Time: The Diary Literature of American Women from 1764 to the Present,* ed. Margo Culley (New York: Feminist Press at CUNY, 1985); Rebecca Hogan, "Engendered Autobiographies: The Diary as a Feminine Form," in *Prose Studies: Special Issue on Autobiography and Questions of Gender* 14.2 (September 1991): 95–107; Cynthia Huff, " 'That Profoundly Female, and Feminist Genre': The Diary as Feminist Praxis," *Women's Studies Quarterly* 17.3–4 (Fall-Winter 1989): 95–106; and Estelle E. Jelinek, "Introduction: Women's Autobiography and the Male Tradition," in *Women's Autobiography: Essays in Criticism,* ed. Estelle E. Jelinek (Bloomington: Indiana U Press, 1980), 1–20, and *The Tradition of Women's Autobiography* (Boston: Twayne, 1986).

[8] Jane H. Hunter describes the instructions often given to young women who kept diaries in "Inscribing the Self in the Heart of the Family: Diaries and Girlhood in Late-Victorian America," *American Quarterly* 44.1 (1992): 51–81.

Notes to 1901 Diary

[1] Mabel's father, Marvin Wait, had given her the 1900 diary for Christmas in 1899. He died five months later, on May 7, 1900.

[2] Fred Roberts, a schoolteacher originally from Potsdam, New York, had left the area for the midwest but wrote regularly to Mabel.

[3] Mabel's older sister Edith was living in Maine with her husband and two children.

[4] It was customary to send local newspapers to correspondents so that they would have some idea of one's surroundings and the local happenings.

[5] Mr. Wait's brother, Allen, and his wife, Mercy, lived in Norwood, about 12 miles from Canton. Mabel visited them frequently.

[6] Irma was the wife of Mabel's brother, Mert. "Taken sick" was a term used for a woman's going into labor.

[7] Crary Mills was a small settlement about three miles from the Wait home.

[8] The Independent Order of Foresters was an insurance organization formed by local farmers to pay sick and retirement benefits. Members paid into it monthly, then drew benefits as they needed them. Some groups also held social functions.

[9] Zuar was Zuar McClellan, the son of a neighbor.

[10] Aunt Laurinda was Mrs. Wait's sister. She and her husband, Jim Thompson, lived in the same neighborhood as the Waits. Aunt Louise was also Mrs. Wait's sister. She and her husband, Nelson Anderson, owned a farm not far from the Waits' in Canton.

[11] Em and Edie were Mabel's cousins, Allen and Mercy Wait's daughters.

[12] Fred was Edie and Em's brother.

[13] Buck's Bridge was a small settlement outside of Canton.

[14] Louisville was a small settlement outside Massena, New York, about 10 miles from Norwood.

[15] W. Elsworth Stedman, *The Yankee Detective: A Drama in Three Acts* (Chicago: T. S. Denison, [?] 1980).

[16] The "common work" was the work one did every day. At Aunt Mercy's it probably involved straightening up the bedroom, preparing breakfast, and cleaning up the kitchen afterward.

[17] Charles Townsend, *Tony the Convict: A Drama in Five Acts* (Chicago: T. S. Denison, 1893).

[18] Charles Townsend, *Uncle Tom's Cabin: A Melodrama in Five Acts* (New York: H. Roorbach, 1889).

[19] Edith's husband, Austin Colson, was a Unitarian minister. The Lenten programs refer to programs for his church.

[20] The Women's Christian Temperance Union often held conventions in local churches and halls to garner support for prohibition.

[21] Mert's wife, Irma, was Irma Carter. Her father was the local blacksmith, and the family were neighbors to the Waits.

[22] The Meads were neighbors who lived on the next road.

[23] Mrs. Wait suffered from inflammatory bowel disease, a gastrointestinal disorder that could have serious consequences. Her attack here is symptomatic of this condition. There are indications throughout the diary that Mabel suffered from the same condition.

[24] Like many people in rural communities in the late nineteenth century, the Waits sometimes traded farm products for goods instead of paying cash.

[25] Charles Monroe Sheldon, *Malcolm Kirk: A Tale of Moral Heroism in Overcoming the World* (London, New York: F. Warne, 1899).

[26] Edith, who wrote poetry, had begun a poem for her mother for Christmas but not finished it. She finished it and sent it to Mabel to place in her mother's hands before the burial.

[27] Estace was Mabel's older cousin, Estace Earl, from Ogdensburg. Uncle Ing was Mrs. Wait's brother who lived in Potsdam. Nellie was his wife.

[28] Mabel's father, Marvin Wait, had died less than a year earlier, and Mabel had also helped to arrange that funeral.

[29] Lena was probably Lena Gardner, a girlfriend of Mabel's. She and her sister Kittie lived with their family in Canton, and Mabel often visited them when she went "down town."

[30] Washing clothes was back-breaking and time-consuming labor. In homes like Mabel's, where there was only limited running water, water had to be carried in from outside, placed in large boilers, heated on the stove, and then placed in a "washing machine," which was operated by hand. Rinse water also had to be carried and heated. Up until this point, Mabel and her mother had done the family wash together.

[31] Since houses were wood and were heated by individual stoves in every room, fires were a constant threat. Many houses and businesses were destroyed by them.

[32] The Pitts and the Endersbees were neighbors.

[33] Mr. Hale was the family lawyer. He had prepared and filed Mr. Wait's will and, presumably, advised the family on other business matters.

[34] The Wait family plot in the Brick Chapel cemetery had a stone monument with the family name engraved on it, and personal names were added as family members died. In addition, individual graves were marked with small stone markers.

[35] The term "receipt" was often used as a synonym for "recipe." The Wait house was lit by kerosene lamps.

[36] "The Universalist Leader" was the official paper of the Universalist Church. It is uncertain to what denomination of the Christian faith the Waits belonged, but Edith was married to a Universalist minister and Mr. Wait had been affiliated with St. Lawrence University which maintained, at the time, a Universalist seminary.

[37] In the winter, people switched from horse-drawn wheeled vehicles to horse-drawn sleighs, which went better over snow. Most of the roads outside of town and all of those in town were dirt, and muddy conditions made travel difficult, particularly in the late winter and early spring.

[38] Little River was a small settlement about a mile from the Wait farm. It was on an alternate route to Canton.

[39] The Taylors lived on the next road.

[40] The Boyden property adjoined the Waits'. The Boydens, like many families in the area, tapped maple trees for the sap. The sugar house was where they boiled the sap down to syrup and stored the syrup after it was prepared.

[41] This is the first mention of many "scenes" between Mabel and Mert on what to do with the farm. When Mr. Wait died he had left the farm equally to his three living children with the proviso that their mother could live on it until her death. After her death, Mert, who had become tired of farming, wanted to sell the farm and take his share of its value to start a new life. Mabel wanted to keep the farm as it was. The argument was complicated by the fact that Mabel did not have the money to buy Mert's share outright and could not handle all the work of the farm herself. It would also have been considered somewhat improper for a young unmarried woman to live alone on a farm with a hired man.

[42] Fred was one of the farm horses, which Mabel drove when she went to town.

[43] "Sugaring off" involved heating maple syrup to a certain temperature, then pouring the warm syrup over snow so that it formed a candy-like substance, which was eaten with spoons. "Warm sugar" often served as the basis for an informal social get together.

[44] "Saturday's work" involved doing all the daily chores and some extra cleaning. Mabel often swept and mopped unused bed chambers on Saturday, cleaned and filled all the kerosene lamps in the house, etc.

[45] Curly was the family dog.

[46] Lee Wallace lived on the main road to Canton, just south of the cemetery.

[47] The Bluetts were neighbors.

[48] The Brick Chapel cemetery, where Mabel's parents were buried, was about a mile from the Wait farm. Mabel often walked there.

[49] The Bullises were neighbors.

[50] Jim Lindley drove a grocery cart. Though Mabel often drove to Crary Mills or to Canton for groceries, town grocers sent men on carts to sell supplies to farms outside town.

[51] "Net" was probably Jeannette Hosley, whose husband George had died in 1900. Her farm was on the main road to Canton, a bit south of the Brick Chapel.

[52] Irving Bacheller, *Eben Holden: A Tale of the North Country* (Boston: Lothrop, 1900).

[53] Mary Johnston, *To Have and To Hold* (Boston and New York: Houghton, Mifflin, 1900).

[54] By 1900, most of the milk produced on dairy farms like the Waits' was taken in cans once or twice a day to small factories, where it was processed along with the milk from other farms and made into cheese or butter. There were several small cheese factories in Canton at the beginning of the twentieth century. The nearest one to the Wait farm was at the end of their road, where it joined the main road to Canton. The Wait mailbox was also on this corner.

[55] A good housewife saved rags until she had a large quantity, then cut them into long strips, braided the strips together, coiled them, and sewed the coils into circular or oval shapes. Braided rugs were the result.

[56] The students were probably from St. Lawrence University in Canton. The campus was about four miles from the Wait farm.

57 Prescott was a town in Canada, directly across the St. Lawrence River from Ogdensburg.

58 Mrs. Poole's husband ran the cheese factory at the end of the Waits' road. Mabel often stopped to visit with the Pooles when she went to the mailbox.

59 "Oilcloths" were probably floor coverings, an early form of linoleum.

60 Mrs. Alexander, *Her Dearest Foe* (London: Macmillan, 1899).

61 Mary Jane Holmes, *Mildred: A Novel* (New York: G. W. Carleton, [1877] 1884).

62 Uncle Austin was Mrs. Wait's brother who lived in Ogdensburg.

63 There was a hospital for the mentally ill in Ogdensburg. Located on the St. Lawrence River, it had lovely grounds and was a favorite spot to walk.

64 When Mert and Irma left the farm, they moved in for a time with Irma's family, the Carters.

65 Patent medicines, which did not require prescriptions, were common. Many women like Mabel, who suffered from chronic headaches and other complaints, bought them from traveling salesmen.

66 Guy was probably Guy Poole, the hired man who took over the farm work after Mert moved.

67 The St. Lawrence County fair was held in Canton, at the fairgrounds located on the Grasse River just north of the village.

68 J. H. Ingraham, *The Prince of the House of David: Or, Three Years in the Holy City* (London: George Routledge and Sons, [1800] 1876).

69 This Latin phrase means, literally, "between the walls." Perhaps Mabel is referring to the fact that she did not go out all day.

70 Mabel's cousin, Bert Earl, had agreed to take on the job of hired man. Part of the agreement included letting Bert and his wife, Lula, and daughter live in the other "part" of the farmhouse once occupied by Mert and Irma. This arrangement both took care of the farm work and silenced those neighbors and family members who were scandalized by Mabel's living alone with a hired man.

71 The Pan American Exhibition, held in Buffalo in 1901, was modeled on the Centennial Exhibition held in Philadelphia in 1876. Its purpose was to further the image of a prosperous U.S. economy and to strengthen business ties with Latin American Countries. Many souvenir cards, plates, spoons, etc. were issued to commemorate it.

72 When a group of men gathered or were hired to do a large farm task like threshing on one farm, it was the responsibility of the farm's housewife to cook for them.

73 Mr. Nichols was probably Charlie, Lula's brother, from Ogdensburg.

74 As the house was heated by individual stoves which were not large enough to hold a fire that would burn all night long, the only way to keep warm at night when the weather was very cold was to stay awake and keep at least one fire going.

75 *Beauties of the Rockies* (Denver: H. H. Tammen Curio Co., 1890).

76 Both Lula's family and Bert's lived in Ogdensburg. Lula was going to spend Christmas with them. Bert joined her after the morning chores on December 25, leaving Mabel alone for Christmas.

Notes to 1902 Diary

[1] Wine plant was another name for rhubarb.

[2] Mr. Conkey was a trustee of St. Lawrence University, the institution that lent Mabel the money to buy Mert's portion of the farm.

[3] This seems to suggest that Charlie Nichols had said he was romantically interested in Mabel. Since there is some evidence in an earlier diary that Fred Roberts had also told Mabel he loved her (July 6, 1900), Nichols' interest put her in the middle of a romantic triangle.

[4] Many small towns had opera houses with large auditoriums, where traveling theater companies, musical groups, and lecturers could put on entertainments for the local populace. The Canton Opera House, a large structure with meeting rooms as well as an auditorium, was located on Main Street.

[5] J. M. Barrie, *The Little Minister* (New York: Grosset & Dunlap, 1892).

[6] Mabel's cousin Eva Earl was a teacher.

[7] Charles F. Coghlan, *The Royal Box* ([New York:] G. W. Kauser Typewriting, 1897).

[8] Leslie Stuart, *Floradora: A Musical Comedy* (London: Francis, Day & Hunter, 1899).

[9] As was a common practice, the neighbor women acted as midwives. No doctor seems to have been present at the birth.

[10] Fannie E. Newberry, *The Wrestler of Philippi: A Tale of the Early Christians* ([Elgin, Ill.:] David C. Cook Pub. Co., 1896).

[11] This is the first direct mention that relatives were talking about Mabel.

[12] Gail Hamilton, *First Love Is Best: A Sentimental Sketch* (Boston: Estes and Lauriat, 1877).

[13] This is the first indication that Fred Roberts was planning to leave St. Louis.

[14] It is clear from this entry that Mabel knew Fred Roberts was planning to return to Canton to see her. Her agitation over what to do suggests that she also knew he was going to press her to decide about their relationship.

[15] Bert and Lula's decision to move out left Mabel once again without a man to do the farm chores. It is worth noticing that Fred Roberts started taking over many of them as soon as he arrived, leading to speculation about whether his arrival was precipitated by Bert's decision to leave.

[16] Mabel's "position," of course, was that she now had no man to do the chores and two men, Charlie Nichols and Fred Roberts, romantically interested in her.

[17] This entry suggests people in Canton were talking about Mabel's situation as an unmarried woman with two suitors who visited her for long periods.

[18] This suggests that Fred Roberts had been pressing Mabel to take this step for some time. Other incidents in the diary, such as Edith's arrival just a few days before his, the round of calls Edith, Mabel, and Fred made in Canton on November 20, and Mabel's flurry to find a dressmaker suggest that Mabel herself had been thinking of the marriage as a probable step.

[19] It is not clear why Mabel was so secretive about the wedding, since she sent out announcements the following week. Weddings at home, however, were fairly common.

[20] Raymondville was a small settlement about five miles from Norwood.

ᨳᢁ Appendix ᨳᢀ

Appendix A

Wait Family Genealogy

I. Herman Wait, b. 1798 ?, d. 1863, m. Margary ?, b. 1836, d. 1882
  A. Allen Wait, d. 1902, m. Mercy ?
    1. Edi Wait
    2. Em Wait, d. 1901
    3. Fred Wait
  B. Marvin R. Wait, b. 1840, d. 1900, m. Almeda Winslow, b. 1841,
        d. 1901
    1. Edith Wait, b. 1865, d. 1942, m. Austin Colson
      a) Carroll Colson, b. 1898 ?
      b) Kathleen Colson, b. 1899, d. 1922
      c) Helene Mabel Colson, b. 1901
    2. Milton Wait, b. 1869, d. 1872
    3. Merton Wait, b. 1873, d. 1922, m. Irma Carter
      a) Maud Wait, b. 1901
      b) Doris Wait
    4. Mabel Wait, b. Oct. 2, 1876, d. Feb. 1936, m. Fred Roberts,
        b. Feb. 29, 1869, d. Feb. 11, 1933
      a) Gladys Wait Roberts, b. Jan. 1908, d. 1991

Winslow Family Genealogy

I. Winslow, m. ?
  A. Almeda Winslow, m. Marvin Wait (see Wait Family Genealogy)
  B. Austin Winslow, m. Susan ?
  C. Louise Winslow, b. 1837, d. 1924, m. Nelson Anderson, b. 1830,
     d. 1912
  D. Laurinda Winslow, m. James Thompson
  E. (Sister) Winslow, m. John Earl
    1. Estace Earl
    2. Eva Earl, b. 1870, d. 1938, m. John Kennedy, b. 1876, d. 1969
      a) Earl Kennedy
    3. Bert Earl, m. Lula Nichols (Charlie Nichols' sister)
      a) Lou Earl
  F. Ing Winslow, m. Nellie

Appendix B

Expenses for January 1901

Jan. 3	4 cts. for postage. 25 cts. for puff comb.
Jan. 5	55 cts. for carfare.
Jan. 7	4 cts. for postage.
Jan. 9	2 cts. for postage.
Jan. 10	2 cts. for postage.
Jan. 11	2 cts. for postage.
Jan. 12	2 cts. for postage. 15 cts. for envelopes.
Jan. 14	4 cts. for postage.
Jan. 16	2 cts. for postage.
Jan. 17	4 cts. for postage.
Jan. 18	25 cts. for play.
Jan. 19	2 cts. for postage. 80 cts. for wrappers.
Jan. 21	2 cts. for postage.
Jan. 23	4 cts. for postage.
Jan. 24	4 cts. for postage.
Jan. 26	2 cts. for postage. 5 cts. for ink.
Jan. 28	4 cts. for postage.
Jan. 29	2 cts. for postage.
Jan. 31	4 cts. for postage.

$2.53 [*sic*] for January.

Expenses for January 1902

Jan. 2	2 cts. for postage.
Jan. 7	6 cts. for postage.
Jan. 9	4 cts. for postage.
Jan. 11	$1.00 for corsets. $2.50 for shoes. 8 cts. for rubber elastic. 20 cts. for ink, pad and envelopes. 25 cts. at post office. $2.05 for "Universalist Leader." 5 cts. for mouse trap. 10 cts. for sheds.
Jan. 13	4 cts. for postage.
Jan. 20	4 cts. for postage.
Jan. 23	4 cts. for postage.
Jan. 27	10 cts. for postage.
Jan. 29	25 cts. for graham. 25 cts. for sugar. 10 cts. for molasses. 35 cts. for coffee. 63 cts. for lard.
Jan. 30	4 cts. for postage.
Jan. 31	$8.19 [*sic*] for January.